Why Do We Say That?

202 Idioms, Phrases, Sayings & Facts! A Brief History On Where They Come From!

Scott Matthews

Copyright © 2022 Scott Matthews

All rights reserved. No part of this publication may be reproduced, distributed or transmitted in any form or by any means, including photocopying, recording, or other electronic or mechanical methods, without the prior written permission of the publisher, except in the case of brief quotations embodied in critical reviews and certain other non-commercial uses permitted by copyright law.

Trademarked names appear throughout this book. Rather than use a trademark symbol with every occurrence of a trademarked name, names are used in an editorial fashion, with no intention of infringement of the respective owner's trademark. The information in this book is distributed on an "as is" basis, without warranty. Although every precaution has been taken in the preparation of this work, neither the author nor the publisher shall have any liability to any person or entity with respect to any loss or damage caused or alleged to be caused directly or indirectly by the information contained in this book.

The more that you read, the more things you will know. The more you learn, the more places you'll go.

- Dr. Seuss

Six Benefits of Reading Idioms

1. Knowledge
2. Stress Reduction
3. Mental Stimulation
4. Better Writing Skills
5. Vocabulary Expansion
6. Better Communication Skills

ABOUT THE AUTHOR

Scott Matthews is a geologist, world traveller and author of the "Amazing World Facts" series! He was born in Brooklyn, New York, by immigrant parents from Ukraine but grew up in North Carolina. Scott studied at Duke University where he graduated with a degree in Geology and History.

His studies allowed him to travel the globe where he saw and learned amazing trivial knowledge with his many encounters. With the vast amount of interesting information he accumulated, he created his best selling books "Random, Interesting & Fun Facts You Need To Know."

He hopes this book will provide you with hours of fun, knowledge, entertainment and laughter.

BONUS!

Thanks for supporting me and purchasing this book! I'd like to send you some freebies. They include:

- The digital version of *500 World War I & II Facts*
- The digital version of *101 Idioms and Phrases*
- The audiobook for my best seller *1144 Random Facts*

Go to the last page of the book and scan the QR code. Enter your email and I'll send you all the files. Happy reading!

Why Do We Say That? is a concise and comprehensive collection of idioms created for you to have an easy-to-use, go-to guide on how to apply and understand the most beautiful aspects of the English language - idioms, popular sayings, phrases, and proverbs.

My goal was to collect idioms, their meanings, uses, and origins so you would have them all in one place and at your hand, instead of having to search the Internet.

Some of these phrases have many uses and can be traced back to numerous origins, countries, and cultures. Since I aim to keep the form short, some of these fascinating stories had to be condensed or even overlooked.

I hope you have fun and grow to love the English language and its rich history even more.

P.S. Apologies to my British friends, I'm using American English rules here so if you see grammatical rules that don't make sense, that's why.

Contents

Book one

1. To turn a blind eye 1
2. Straight from the horse's mouth 2
3. Caught red-handed 3
4. To eat humble pie 4
5. To pull out all the stops 5
6. The writing is on the wall 6
7. To let the cat out of the bag 7
8. To bite the bullet 8
9. To break the ice 9
10. Rule of thumb 10
11. A grain of salt 12
12. To run amuck 13
13. To butter someone up 14
14. To cost an arm and a leg 15
15. Cat got your tongue? 16
16. Burning the midnight oil 17
17. Off the record 18
18. To paint the town red 19
19. To bury the hatchet 20
20. Riding shotgun 21
21. To give the cold shoulder 23
22. To let your hair down 24
23. Chew the fat 25
24. To pull someone's leg 26
25. To steal one's thunder 27
26. A bigwig 28
27. Red herring 29
28. One for the road 30
29. Don't look a gift horse in the mouth 31
30. To kick the bucket 32
31. A different kettle of fish 34
32. A king's ransom 35
33. To read the riot act 36
34. Once in a blue moon 37
35. A fly in the ointment 38
36. Blue blood 39
37. Fly off the handle 40
38. Resting on laurels 41
39. White elephant 42
40. To learn the ropes 43
41. A feather in one's cap 45
42. A bird in hand 46
43. It rained cats and dogs 47

44. A shot in the arm 48
45. To use a sledgehammer to crack a nut 49
46. A red rag to a bull 50
47. Till the cows come home 51
48. To go the whole nine yards 52
49. Achilles heel 53
50. To spill the beans 54
51. Ace in the hole 56
52. The acid test 57
53. Abracadabra 58
54. Hold a candle to something 59
55. Rub the wrong way 60
56. A baker's dozen 61
57. Cut to the chase 62
58. Above board 63
59. Wet blanket 64
60. Not for all the tea in China 65
61. All at sea 67
62. Namby pamby 68
63. Beat around the bush 69
64. To pass with flying colors 70
65. As dead as a dodo 71
66. To get cold feet 72
67. As mad as a hatter 73
68. As happy as a clam 74
69. As easy as pie 75
70. Dead ringer 76
71. As the crow flies 78
72. To give something a wide berth 79
73. As thick as thieves 80
74. At loggerheads 81
75. The whole shebang 82
76. Young Turks 83
77. Bells and whistles 84
78. Below the belt 85
79. Have your work cut out for you 86
80. Basket case 87
81. Sleep tight 89
82. Put a sock in it 90
83. Goody two shoes 91
84. Crocodile tears 92
85. Ball and chain 93
86. In the limelight 94
87. Bail out 95
88. Show your true colors 96
89. The walls have ears 97

90. Push the envelope 98
91. Badger to death 100
92. Saved by the bell 101
93. Armed to the teeth 102
94. To go haywire 103
95. Barking up the wrong tree 104
96. Hear something through the grapevine 105
97. Hands down 106
98. Run of the mill 107
99. Break a leg 108
100. Get on a soapbox 109
101. Honeymoon 110

Book two
1. All roads lead to Rome 113
2. Mark my words 114
3. Paddle your own canoe 115
4. Make a mountain out of a molehill 116
5. In a pickle 117
6. No dice 118
7. Harp on 119
8. In cold blood 120
9. When pigs fly 121
10. Stir up a hornet's nest 122
11. Joined at the hip 124
12. Knock on wood 125
13. Fat chance 126
14. A smooth sea never made a skilled sailor 127
15. In the loop 128
16. Miss the boat 129
17. Get the wrong end of the stick 130
18. Ahead of the curve 131
19. Back to square one 132
20. Bull in a china shop 133
21. Mind your own beeswax 135
22. No spring chicken 136
23. Across the board 137
24. Stand your ground 138
25. Everything but the kitchen sink 139
26. Drop like flies 140
27. Every cloud has a silver lining 141
28. A stitch in time saves nine 142
29. Kick the can down the road 143
30. Call the shots 144
31. On the cards 146

32. Knock your socks off 147
33. A bed of roses 148
34. In a nutshell 149
35. Walking on eggshells 150
36. Spanner in the works 151
37. Brownie points 152
38. Fair and square 153
39. Laughing stock 154
40. Keep your nose clean 155
41. Elephant in the room 157
42. Green thumb 158
43. Jump on the bandwagon 159
44. An ace up one's sleeve 160
45. Out on the town 161
46. Wouldn't be caught dead 162
47. Born with a silver spoon in your mouth 163
48. Fan the flames 164
49. Down to the wire 165
50. Bare bones 166
51. In the nick of time 168
52. At odds 169
53. Hissy fit 170
54. The devil is beating his wife 171
55. Add fuel to the fire 172
56. Buckle down 173
57. Red tape 174
58. On top of the world 175
59. Pay the piper 176
60. Play cat and mouse 177
61. Let the chips fall where they may 179
62. Mumbo jumbo 180
63. Loose cannon 181
64. A slap on the wrist 182
65. Low hanging fruit 183
66. Head over heels 184
67. The eleventh hour 185
68. Hot Potato 186
69. Old habits die hard 187
70. In mint condition 188
71. Green with envy 190
72. Cut the cord 191
73. Keen as mustard 192
74. Dead as a doornail 193
75. Tall story 194
76. Hit or miss 195
77. Rain or shine 196

78. Fight tooth and nail 197
79. Piece of cake 198
80. Where the rubber meets the road 199
81. Square peg in a round hole 201
82. Pep talk 202
83. Pie in the sky 203
84. Bob's your uncle 204
85. All ears 205
86. Night owl 206
87. Jack of all trades 207
88. Chew the fat 208
89. On the mend 209
90. Jump the gun 210
91. Halfway house 212
92. Bull's eye 213
93. On a tear 214
94. Read between the lines 215
95. Leg it 216
96. Mum's the word 217
97. Means to an end 218
98. Devil's advocate 219
99. Once bitten twice shy 220
100. To the nines 221
101. When in rome 222
Bonus 224

Book one

1. To Turn a Blind Eye

The phrase "to turn a blind eye," which means to ignore something, comes from a British admiral who actually had one blind eye. Back in 1801, during the Battle of Copenhagen, Admiral Horatio Nelson received flag signals from his fleet commander Admiral Sir Hyde Parker, ordering him to stop an attack on enemy ships. Using his one blind eye, Admiral Nelson pretended to look through his telescope, and then declared to his men that he didn't see the flag signals. Nelson continued with the attack, succeeded, and was promoted to fleet commander after Parker was fired.

2. Straight from the horse's mouth

Horse racing is a pastime that dates back to 12th century Britain and it's especially popular with punters (gamblers). To increase their chances of winning wagers, punters usually share tips about the horses' traits. The most trusted tips are those from people like horse trainers and stable lads because they are closest to the horses. Such tips were said to be "straight from the horse's mouth," because the tipsters had a direct connection to the horse. Today, that expression is commonly used to indicate that certain information is to be trusted because it comes from the person or entity who's best placed to know the facts.

3. Caught red-handed

The idiom "caught red-handed," which means to be caught while in the process of doing something wrong, originated in Scotland in the 15th century. It was coined in reference to an old English law that was established to punish people who butchered stolen farm animals. According to the law, for a suspect to be convicted, he had to be found with the butchered animal's blood still on his hands.

4. To Eat Humble Pie

Back in the 14th century, after hunting parties returned home, the lords and other important men were offered the finest cuts of meat, while men of lower social stature were offered the entrails of the animals. These entrails were known as "numbles," a term that was shortened to "umbles" by the 15th century. Often, the "umbles" (pronounced as "humble") were baked into pies and served to the low-class men who considered it a humiliation. That's how the idiom "to eat humble pie" came about. Today, it means to accept that you are wrong and to apologize.

5. To pull out all the stops

Pipe organs are musical instruments that produce sound by pushing pressurized air through pipes. The pipes have knobs that control the tone and volume of the instrument. These knobs are known as "stops," and when they are pulled out, the instrument can play all tones at the same time and produce the highest volume possible. This is the origin of the idiom "to pull out all the stops," which means to make the maximum possible effort to achieve something.

6. The Writing is on the Wall

We use the idiom "the writing is on the wall" to mean that a certain result has become inevitable, or that a potentially dangerous situation has become imminent and unavoidable. This phrase originates from the Bible, specifically in the book of Daniel. Belshazzar, a corrupt, unjust, and unworthy king, was debasing sacred objects and spending his time drinking and revelling instead of leading his people. During one such debauchery-filled event, a disembodied hand (supposedly the hand of God) appeared and wrote an ominous warning on the palace wall. The prophet Daniel was brought in to interpret the writing, and he explained that God had passed jugement on the king and his kingdom, found them wanting, and decided to break the kingdom apart and hand over control to foreigners. The writing on the wall was effectively a final judgement, one that the king had no power to get around – it was inevitable.

7. TO LET THE CAT OUT OF THE BAG

Back in the early 16th century, in medieval markets, traders would sell piglets tied up inside sacks to make it much easier for farmers to transport them back to their farms. Farmers usually wouldn't bother opening the sack to confirm their purchase because they didn't want to have to chase a loose piglet around the crowded market. So, some shady dealers came up with an idea to swindle unsuspecting farmers. They would find less valuable animals such as cats, tie them in bags, and try to con farmers into buying them. If the farmer chose to open the bag, the jig was up. That's the origin of the expression "to let the cat out of the bag," which we use today to mean to reveal a secret, either intentionally or unintentionally.

8. To bite the bullet

Before the development of anesthetics, surgeries were painful affairs, especially when performed on the battlefield. When soldiers were wounded, they had to be stitched up, or even get limbs amputated, as quickly as possible in crude and very painful processes. Sometimes, the pain would be so overwhelming that the soldier in question would grind his teeth and bite his tongue. To prevent this, the soldier would be given a pad of leather or a wooden stick to bite on as the procedure was being performed. However, there were instances when things moved so fast, and the battlefield was so chaotic, that no one had the time to find a pad or a stick. In those cases, someone would pop a bullet out of a rifle and give it to the soldier to bite on. That's how the expression "to bite the bullet" came about. It means to accept a hardship that's inevitable or to endure impending pain with courage and resilience.

9. To Break the Ice

For centuries, navigation has been a great challenge, particularly in icy waters. That's why the expression "to break the ice" has been used in the English language as far back as the 16th century. At that time, sailors would use hand tools to dig through the ice to create a path for small boats; people adapted "breaking the ice" to figuratively mean to forge a path for others to follow. Two centuries later, as navigation became more advanced, special ships known as "ice-breakers" were introduced. These ships went ahead of others and used their strong hulls and powerful engines to crush ice and create waterways for other vessels. That's how "breaking the ice" came to mean smoothing out a socially awkward situation in order to establish a free, relaxed, and open relationship or dynamic.

10. Rule of Thumb

The phrase "rule of thumb" refers to a way to evaluate something based on rough estimates or practical instructions, as opposed to precise measurements or scientific principles. It's a common and handy phrase, but it has unsavory origins. Back in the day, under English common law, a man was given a legal right to chastise his wife through corporal punishment, but this was allowed in moderation. Legend has it that an 18th century judge by the name of Sir Francis Buller made a legal determination that a man could hit his wife with a stick, as long as the stick was no thicker than his thumb.

Did you know?

When you sprinkle a pineapple with salt, it becomes sweeter. It's because table salt is mainly sodium chloride, and the sodium is effective in lowering bitterness levels in foods. Scientists have found that salt diminishes our tongues' perception of the sour taste that's caused by the acidity of some foods, and this allows the sweetness of the food to feature more prominently in our taste palates.

Portobello, cremini, and button mushrooms are actually the same type of mushroom, just at different stages of maturity. After the Agaricus bisporus species sprouts, they first grow into a button mushroom. If they aren't harvested at the button stage, they will turn brown and grow into cremini mushrooms. If they still aren't harvested at this stage, they will keep growing into large and fully mature portobello mushrooms. This one species of mushroom accounts for 90% of all mushrooms produced in the US.

Rats have been known to multiply very quickly. In fact, scientists estimate that in a span of just a year and a half, two rats can have more than one million descendants!

11. A Grain of Salt

A long time ago, in 77 AD, a scholar named Pliny the Elder translated an ancient recipe that was used as an antidote to poison. At the end of the recipe, he wrote that it should be taken "plus a grain of salt." The concoction consisted mostly of nasty herbs and the grain of salt was meant to make it easier to swallow. This text came to be understood by future scholars (at least in the metaphorical sense) to mean that serious injurious effects can be avoided or at least moderated by taking a grain of salt. Also, as people learned more about the effects of poison on the body over the centuries, it became increasingly clear that Pliny's antidote didn't have the healing powers it claimed to have, so it was wise to take his advice with a bit of skepticism. So, his famous line "a grain of salt" became synonymous with "a degree of skepticism." Today, the expression to take something with "a grain of salt" or "a pinch of salt" means to consider or accept the information that's being offered to you, while at the same time maintaining some level of skepticism as to how true that information might be.

12. To run amuck

Back in the 15th and 16th centuries in Southeast Asia, there were warriors known as the Amuco. These were "death or glory" warriors who believed that if they died in battle, they became the favorites of the gods, and that it was preferable to die fighting than to accept defeat. They fought for different factions in the power struggles in Malaysia and Java, and they were known for their drug-induced maniacal and frenzied attacks. When they fought in an area, they would run into houses, kill almost everyone they met, and leave utter chaos in their wake. Legends of the Amuco warriors spread to Europe, and the expression "to run amok" or "to run amuck" was adapted into English with the meaning to go crazy or to behave in an extremely wild or unruly manner.

13. TO BUTTER SOMEONE UP

In ancient India, people would throw little pieces of ghee butter at the statues of some of their gods when praying for personal favors. In Tibetan traditional practices, they would craft sculptures of divine figures from butter during the New Year festivities, a ritual that was meant to bring peace, happiness, and prosperity in the coming year. In both these instances, butter was associated with flattery. Today, the expression "to butter someone up" means to flatter, praise, compliment or charm someone. Just like in ancient India, the goal of buttering someone up is to gain favor from them.

14. To Cost an Arm and a Leg

Many centuries ago, before photography was invented, people would hire painters to draw their portraits. Portrait painting is an involving and expensive art form, so the larger and more detailed the portrait was, the more it cost. It became common for people of limited means to prefer to have just their head and shoulders painted as opposed to the whole body. Only royals and other rich patrons could afford portraits that included arms and legs. That was the birth of the phrase "to cost an arm and a leg," which means to cost an exorbitant amount of money. Later, in the 19th and 20th centuries, soldiers would lose their limbs in war, and "an arm and a leg" took on a more literal meaning because many considered the loss of body parts too high a price to pay.

15. Cat got your tongue?

When someone goes inexplicably silent when you expect them to speak, it's common to nudge them with the light-hearted question "cat got your tongue?" That question wasn't always asked with a light touch. It's the shortened version of the question "has the cat got your tongue?" which originates from the old British military. Back in the day, those who were found guilty of wrongdoing were flogged. There was a specially made whip called "the cat o' nine tails" which captains would use to whip the errant individuals. The whip had nine braided lashes that were designed to inflict multiple wounds. It was sometimes called "the cat" because it would produce wounds that looked like cat scratches. The people who had the misfortune of being flogged were so stunned that they were unable to speak for a while, so other people would mock them by asking if the cat had got their tongue.

16. Burning the Midnight Oil

Long before electricity, natural gas, and fossil fuels were utilized, people used candles and oil lamps to light up their homes at night. Oil was very expensive because it was sourced from whales. So, it was common for people to use their oil sparingly. They would try to wind down their activities early in the evening so that they could put out their lamps and retire to bed. Once in a while, people had activities that were so important or urgent that they had to keep working on them late into the night despite the high cost of whale oil. That is why, in the 17th century, people started referring to late night work as "burning the midnight oil." Today, we no longer use oil lamps, but the phrase is still used in reference to late night study sessions or overnight work on projects with upcoming deadlines.

17. Off the Record

When someone says something "off the record," it means that they are sharing information in confidence, and there is an agreement that whatever they are saying should either not be repeated to other people, or if it's repeated, it should not be attributed to the original speaker. This phrase was inadvertently coined by President Franklin Roosevelt in 1932. At the time, interviews were conducted and recorded in very formal settings, and by saying that he wanted to speak off the record, Roosevelt meant that he wanted to talk to journalists and audiences in a more laid back setting where he could crack a few jokes rather than just focus on serious topics. The term quickly gained popularity among journalists who started to classify their interviews as "on the record," where people officially acknowledged their statements, and "off the record," where the identity of informers remained confidential.

18. To Paint the Town Red

The Marquis of Waterford, a man named Henry de la Poer Beresford, was well known for his wild partying and mischief. The public referred to him as "the Mad Marquis" because he was known for getting kicked out of Oxford University, getting into crazy fights that sometimes ended in duels, stealing, and damaging property. In one of his most legendary rampages, the Marquis visited the town of Melton Mowbray with a bunch of his friends. He got really drunk and somehow ended up painting several buildings in the town red. His spree became a matter of public obsession at the time, and that's how the phrase "to paint the town red" came to mean to go out and enjoy oneself in a flamboyant or over the top manner.

19. To bury the hatchet

Native American tribes used to engage in long and brutal battles against each other. They used a variety of weapons including special types of axes known as hatchets. Occasionally, the chiefs of warring tribes would meet to try to strike up a peace agreement. In cases where a peace accord was arrived upon, a ceremony would be held to mark the occasion. Warriors from both sides of the conflict would dig up a hole, toss in their weapons (including their hatchets), and cover them all with dirt before the festivities continued. This was meant to symbolize that the tribes were burying the animosity between them. The phrase "to bury the hatchet" was borrowed from this Native American tradition. It's now used to mean to settle one's differences with an adversary.

20. Riding shotgun

Once upon a time in the Wild West, long before the automobile was invented, people used to traverse the wild terrain in stagecoaches. This was a dangerous journey, not just because of the unknown geography and wild animals, but also because of highway bandits and hostile natives. To protect the stagecoach, the person sitting next to the driver had to be armed with a shotgun. After automobiles were invented, riding in the front passenger seat became known as "riding shotgun." This phrase stuck in part because of the numerous western movies of the early 20th century which commonly depicted those wild stagecoach rides.

DID YOU KNOW?

"Shat mat" is an Arabic expression that means "the king is dead" and it's the origin of the term checkmate. The game of chess existed in the East in many different forms since the sixth century, and it reached Europe via the Arab world. The term "mate" in the word "checkmate" has nothing to do with the English word which means friend or companion. Instead, it's true meaning is more closely related to the modern Persian word "mate" which means "unresponsive" or "unable to respond."

Most gladiators were vegetarians. Their diets consisted mainly of barley and vegetables. Just like modern athletes, gladiators needed to replenish their electrolytes and to fortify their bodies after physical exertion during fights. Anthropological evidence shows that they used to make health-boosting tonic drinks from plant ashes.

During Roman times, salt used to be highly scarce and very valuable, and it was referred to as "white gold." Salt was valuable because it was used to preserve perishable foods, particularly meat and fish. In fact, Roman soldiers were sometimes paid with salt instead of money. These wages were known as "salarium," a word whose root is "sal" which is the Latin word for salt. This word later evolved into "salaire" in French and eventually it became the English word "salary."

21. To Give the Cold Shoulder

To give someone a cold shoulder means to treat them with aloofness or even disdain. We use it to refer to any unfriendly or passively hostile response that one could give to someone else, perhaps because of indifference or a clear intent to hurt the other person's feelings. Back in the day, giving a "cold shoulder" had a similar meaning, but it was more literal. According to folk stories, it was common for visitors to show up unannounced. If the hosts were pleasantly surprised to see the visitors, they would take their time to prepare a nice hot meal for them. However, if they were displeased or considered the visit an intrusion, they couldn't kick the guest out because hospitality was customary, so the hosts expressed their displeasure by serving the guests a cold shoulder of mutton.

22. To let your hair down

Back in the 17th century, aristocratic women were required to present the best possible image during social events. They dressed up in elegant gowns and their hair would be styled and pinned up whenever they had to appear in public. Some even wore tiaras, pins, or elegant hats to show their class. It would be considered an embarrassment if the hair came apart in public, so the aristocratic women had to walk around like stills, avoiding any fun or physically demanding activities that could dishevel their hair. This meant that although the women looked elegant, they were unable to feel free and relaxed. It was only when these women got back to their private quarters that they could unpin their hair either to wash and brush it or just to feel relaxed. That's how the phrase "to let one's hair down" came to mean to relax and to act in a free or uninhibited manner.

23. CHEW THE FAT

The expression to "chew the fat" means to make friendly small talk with people, in the form of a long, informal conversation among friends or even a gossip session. Chewing the fat came to be synonymous with idle chit chat because, centuries ago in Britain, people would actually snack on fatty pork rind while idly chatting away. Farmers would preserve their pork by smoking and salting it, and when their friends paid them informal visits to talk about mundane things, they would offer them pieces of fatty pork rind. This practice was also common in the royal navy. After spending some time at sea, and when the food reserves were running low, sailors were served with fatty, salty pork rind, which they took with them out of the dining area and chewed on as they chatted when they had free time. The practice of chewing on fat died off with time, but the expression stuck around.

24. To pull someone's leg

During the Middle Ages in Britain, thieves would use all forms of trickery to target their victims. Some thieves worked in small teams. They would blend into the crowd and one would find a way of confusing the target while the others took off with his or her belongings. In one iteration of this con, a thief would pretend to be a beggar or a trader, or he would hide in a corner. He would then grab on to the leg of the intended victim and pull on it until the victim fell on the ground. His friends would then swoop in, rob the victim, and they would all vanish into the crowd before the victim had time to raise any alarm. Retellings of such robberies would elicit laughs from people because of their comical nature. That's how the expression "pulling one's leg" came to mean deceiving someone in a funny or playful way.

25. To steal one's thunder

Back in the early 18th century, a man named John Dennis tried his hand on producing plays, but they weren't very successful as they didn't resonate with audiences. For one play called *Appius and Virginia*, Dennis devised a technically advanced method of producing the sound of thunder on stage. His thunder was certainly dramatic and brilliant, but that wasn't enough to make people like his play, so he had to shut it down. A while later, when Dennis went to the theater to see a production of Macbeth, he was astonished to realize that they were using his method to produce the sound of thunder. While expressing his dismay, Dennis is quoted as having said "Damn them! They will not let my play run, but they steal my thunder!" That's how the expression "to steal one's thunder" came about. It means to use someone's ideas or creations for one's own advantage, or to prevent someone from getting well deserved success or recognition for their work.

26. A BIGWIG

Back in the 17th century, it was fashionable for people to shave their heads and wear wigs in place of their hair. Originally, this was done because men wanted to sport bold hair styles that weren't attainable with their natural hair. Among the more enlightened people at the time, it was a statement of triumph of human ingenuity over nature. Because the hair used to make the wigs was expensive and scarce, wigs quickly became a status symbol. Men of limited means were seen wearing wigs made of just a few strands of hair. On the other hand, wealthy and influential men were able to purchase massive wigs that were made up of thousands of hair strands. People could immediately tell how rich you were based on the size of your wig. People started referring to rich men as "bigwigs." This fashion trend faded away after the top-hat became popular, but wigs are still used ceremonially in the judiciary and legislature in Britain and other commonwealth nations. To date, the term "bigwigs" is still used in reference to important, influential, or high status people.

27. Red herring

A "red herring" refers to something such as a clue that is deliberately meant to be distracting or misleading. It is mostly used in detective stories to talk about false leads that investigators waste time pursuing. The expression comes from the name given to smoked herring fish, which is called red herring because the smoking process has the effect of turning it red. In the 17th century, red herring was mostly consumed by members of the lower classes. Hunters often used their hounds to hunt for small animals such as hares. The problem was that these hounds would sometimes catch animals that belonged to poor farmers out in the country instead of wild ones. To protect their animals from hunters and their hounds, the farmers would hide red herring deep in the woods. The hounds would pursue the strong scent of the red herring over long distances instead of looking for prey, and the hunters would be disappointed to find red herring at the end of their trek.

28. One for the Road

The phrase "one for the road" refers to the common practice of taking one last drink before leaving on a journey. In old England, pubs were few and far between, so it was common for people to gulp down a final pint of beer before hitting the road because they knew it would be a while before they would enjoy another refreshing drink. That's how the expression "one for the road" came about. There's also an old legend that explains an older and more sinister use of the expression. The story goes that condemned men would often be transported from the Newgate prison to Tyburn where they were to be hanged. Those transporting the prisoners often took pity on them, so a tradition emerged where they would stop at a tavern along the route and the condemned men would be allowed to have one last drink.

29. Don't look a gift horse in the mouth

Long before vehicles were invented, horses were the most reliable means of transportation, which made them extremely valuable. The average person at that time knew more about horses than the average person today. For example, when buying a horse, you would be able to tell its age by looking into its mouth and counting its teeth. A horse with fewer teeth might not be old enough, while one with damaged teeth might be too old. Examining a horse's mouth was an easy way to know more about it. However, if the horse in question was presented as a gift, it would be very insulting to the person giving it away if the recipient of the horse looked in its mouth right in front of them. That's where the English proverb "don't look a gift horse in the mouth" comes from. It means that if someone offers you a gift or does you a favor, you should not react in a manner that suggests you are ungrateful, or that you don't trust the quality of their offering.

30. To Kick the Bucket

"Kicking the bucket" is a colloquial and rather indifferent term for dying. Many people assume that the word "bucket" in the phrase "to kick the bucket" refers to a pail, a container for transporting liquids, but actually it doesn't. In Old English, "bucket" had another meaning. It referred to a special kind of yoke that they would use to hold pigs up in the air by their hind legs while they were being slaughtered. This yoke looked similar to the pulley that's used to draw water from wells, and its name was derived from the old French word "buquet" which translates to "a balance" in modern English. In the moments before they died, the pigs would spasm and move violently, kicking the bucket as though they were trying to get free. Sixteenth century farmers started saying "kicking the bucket" in reference to people passing away as a way to make light of news that saddened them.

Did you know?

In the past, the main purpose of marriage was to procreate, so Romans used to shower the new bride with fertility symbols like wheat grain. This wheat used to be baked into small cakes to be eaten in a tradition known as confarreatio, meaning to eat together. The guests of the ceremony used to throw handfuls of honey-eyed nuts and dried fruits called confetto, which gave birth to the tradition of throwing confetti at weddings. Although the throwing of confetti started out as a pagan tradition, it was slowly interpreted into Christian celebrations such as church weddings and baptisms. Today, confetti comes in many forms and is used to celebrate many kinds of events, including sporting events, parades, etc.

The word zip in "zip code" is actually an acronym for Zone Improvement Plan. ZIP codes were introduced and marketed by the US Postal Service because they needed a system that would make it possible to sort mail automatically.

31. A Different Kettle of Fish

For centuries, people in England and Scotland have used special kinds of nets known as kettle nets on fishing expeditions. When these nets are pulled from the water, they come out very messy. The fish are entangled with seaweed, logs, dirt, and lots of unwanted creatures that get caught up in the mix. Fishermen would have a difficult time sorting the fish from the mess. That's the origin of the expression "a pretty kettle of fish" which means an awkward and completely muddled state of affairs. This expression is often confused with another related expression "a different kettle of fish." The latter expression evolved from the former one much more recently. "A different kettle of fish" means a whole other messy or awkward issue than the one you had already agreed to deal with.

32. A king's ransom

Some aspects of medieval warfare were conducted like businesses. For instance, influential people who were captured by the enemy had price tags put on their head in the form of ransom money. The richer the person in question, the higher the ransom that could be asked for. Armies were offered bonuses if they captured high value individuals such as lords or even kings. The king's ransom was higher than that of anyone else for the obvious reason that kings were the richest, most powerful people at the time. In one instance, in 1192, King Richard I of England was captured by the Duke of Austria, and a ransom of 100,000 silver pounds had to be paid before he was released. That's how the phrase "a king's ransom" came to mean an exceedingly large sum of money.

33. To Read the Riot Act

Back in 18th century England, the government was afraid of the Jacobite movement which sought to replace the monarchy with another bloodline through violent means. The Jacobites often gathered in mobs and started riots. A new law called the riot act was passed to help deal with the mobs. If a suspicious looking group of twelve or more people were gathered anywhere, the local magistrate would show up and literally read the riot act to the rowdy mob. If the group did not disperse by onc hour after the reading, they would be arrested and severely punished. Throughout the 18th century, the phrase "reading the riot act" had a literal meaning. It wasn't until the early 19th century that it started to take on a figurative meaning. Today, "to read the riot act to someone" means to reprimand or to call out a person, and to warn them to stop behaving badly.

34. Once in a blue moon

When you say something occurs "once in a blue moon" it means that it happens rarely. That's how the expression is used today, although that wasn't always the case. Originally, the term "blue moon" was meant to express an absurdity, something that sounded too ridiculous to be true. Critics of the church published a pamphlet back in the 16th century where they argued that people shouldn't assume something is true just because a cleric said it. They reasoned that if a priest said the moon was blue, only fools and gullible people would believe them. The words "blue moon" were used in literary works in the 19th century to mean "long and lonely month" and that's when the phrase took on its current meaning. Later, in the 20th century, astrologists redefined the term "blue moon" to mean "the second full moon in a calendar month." There are historical records of nights when the moon did in fact appear blue, most notably after the 1883 Krakatoa volcanic eruption.

35. A Fly in the Ointment

Today, ointments are mostly known for their medicinal uses, but centuries ago, they had multiple applications. Ointments were special creams and oils that were used for a wide range of cosmetic and ceremonial applications. In religious ceremonies, ointments were used to anoint people. These ointments were concocted from organic materials, which had smells that would attract flies. If an ointment was left out in the open, flies would sometimes land on it and die, spoiling the whole batch in the process. This was a common occurrence, and it's even noted in the Bible in the book of Ecclesiastes, which has a passage that says "dead flies cause the ointment of the apothecary to send forth a stink…" That's the origin of the English expression "a fly in the ointment" which means a small but irritating flaw, problem or complication that effectively spoils the entire thing. Often, it's used in instances where a plan seems to be going well, until a very small revelation throws everything into shambles.

36. Blue blood

For centuries in Europe, it was considered important for people of royal blood and other aristocratic families to avoid intermarrying with people of other races and ethnicities, to maintain the quality of their bloodlines. You could tell how pure a royal was depending on how pale his or her skin was, those with pale skin had veins that were more visible than those with darker skin. Furthermore, when veins are viewed through pale skin, the blood inside seems to have a bluish hue. In 18th century Spain, the Castile aristocratic family was particularly proud of the fact that they, unlike some other families, had never intermarried with the Moors or other races, and people started referring to them as "sangre azul" which is Spanish for "blue blood." In the 19th century, the phrase became popular, and people started using it to refer to all nobles and aristocrats, irrespective of how pale their skin was. Today, the term is used to describe all kinds of people that come from privileged, wealthy or powerful families.

37. Fly off the handle

Before saw mills and other timber processing machinery were invented, people had to rely on good old axes to cut down trees, split firewood, and do many other tasks around their farms. These axes had iron heads and they were fitted with wooden handles. After prolonged use, the axe heads would become loose, and if they were not refastened, they could literally fly off the handle mid-swing. This would pose serious danger to the person swinging the axe, other people working or standing near him, or farm animals grazing nearby. Axes that flew off the handle always created dangerous situations. That's how the phrase "to fly off the handle" came to mean to lose one's temper or self-control in a sudden or unexpected way or to get suddenly enraged and to behave in a risky or dangerous manner.

38. Resting on laurels

Sweet bay trees, scientifically known as Laurus nobilis, are currently cultivated for their culinary and ornamental value, but they have been used to make sweet-smelling decorative wreaths since ancient Greece. These wreaths were known as laurels and they were used to symbolize status and victory. In Greek mythology, there's a tale of the god Apollo falling in love with a nymph named Daphne. When Apollo approached Daphne, his power made her turn into a sweet bay tree, so Apollo in his grief, cut a branch off the tree, wore it on his head as a wreath, and declared the tree sacred. For centuries, Greeks, Romans, and Europeans would give laurel wreaths to sports champions and other remarkable people who were then referred to as "laureates." That, in part, explains why Nobel Prize winners are called laureates. That is also the origin of the English expression "to rest on one's laurels," which means to be satisfied with past successes, and to choose to relax instead of making any further effort. The expression is used to criticize people who have had great success in the past, and choose to ride on those successes instead of continuing to work hard.

39. WHITE ELEPHANT

Albino elephants, also known as white elephants, were considered sacred in many Asian countries, particularly in Thailand. People who were charged with taking care of these white elephants were required to provide them with special kinds of foods, groom and decorate them with special jewelry, and keep them in nice places that were accessible to people who wanted to visit the elephants to worship them. As a result, keeping a white elephant became such an expressive affair that only a few people could manage to do it. At some point, the Thai king figured out that he could use white elephants to punish people that displeased him. If he was dissatisfied with a subordinate, he would offer that individual a white elephant as a gift. The individual had no choice but to accept the elephant and to spend all of his resources taking care of it, because doing otherwise would be both sacrilegious and offensive to his king. Some of the people who were gifted with white elephants ended up in financial ruin. That's how the expression "a white elephant" came to mean a burdensome possession that created more disadvantages than advantages. Today, we mostly use the expression to refer to big projects that are abandoned after a lot of money has been spent on them.

40. To learn the ropes

Long before the advent of steam engines, most water vessels were wind-powered. Before someone could be considered a seasoned or qualified sailor, they had to learn the correct way of raising, rigging, and securing the wind sails on the specific boat or ship on which they were to serve. Much of this involved knowing which ropes were associated with which outcomes as far as the sails were concerned. They also needed to learn to tie and untie different kinds of knots. That's how the phrase "to learn the ropes" or "to know the ropes" came to mean to be well acquainted with all the specific methods needed to perform a function. After it had been in use in the nautical world for centuries, the phrase found some more literal use in theaters where ropes were used in stage control to draw curtains and raise scenes. Today, the phrase is mostly used figuratively when someone is learning a new skill.

Did you know?

The reason why t-shirts are called that is because they are shaped like a "t" when laid down. Originally, T-shirts were crew-neck undergarments only worn by men, but today, T-shirts come in many styles and fabrics, and are worn both as inner and outerwear by both males and females.

In honor of Roman dictator Julius Caesar, the month of July was named after him. He actually helped develop the Julian calendar, which is the precursor to the Gregorian calendar that we use today. Before and during Julius Caesar's lifetime, July was known as "Quintilis" which means "the fifth month" because the year used to start in March, and January and February weren't yet part of the calendar. After he was assassinated in 44 BC, the Romans renamed July, his birth month, in his honor.

Hopscotch, the popular playground game, actually dates back to ancient Britain, when the Isles were under the Roman Empire. It started out as a military training exercise for Roman soldiers. The courts were originally quite large, at about 100 feet (thirty meters) long. The soldiers would run through the courts while wearing their full armor and carrying heavy bags in order to improve their footwork. Children were fascinated by this exercise, so they started drawing their own smaller courts and coming up with their own rules for the game. The game spread to different countries across Europe, and later to other parts of the world.

41. A FEATHER IN ONE'S CAP

Because of their beautiful shapes and colors, bird's feathers have been used for decorative purposes in many cultures around the world. In some cultures, when bird feathers were used to decorate headgear, they had a specific symbolic meaning. For example, in some Native American tribes, warriors wore headgear made of feathers, and they were allowed to add one new feather for every enemy combatant they killed. Warriors in Mongolia and Hungary also had similar practices. In the British Isles, particularly in Scotland and Wales, it was customary for hunters who killed their first woodcocks to pull out a feather from the bird and stick it in their hats. Across history and culture, the addition of feathers to one's hat or headgear would symbolize someone's prowess, either as a hunter or a warrior. That's where the English idiom "a feather in one's cap" comes from. It's commonly used today to mean any admirable achievement or success by an individual, which can be used to boost one's reputation and improve their standing with their peers.

42. A Bird in Hand

In medieval England, falconry was commonly used as a hunting technique. This is a practice where birds of prey, including falcons, hawks and eagles, are trained to catch small prey such as rabbits and squirrels. These birds weren't particularly easy to train. They often scratched the trainers or took the prey for themselves. It took a lot of effort to domesticate a bird of prey and teach it to be a reliable hunting companion. So, once a bird had been fully trained, its value would increase for all practical purposes. Among falconers, it became accepted wisdom that it was better to have one trained bird than several wild untrained ones straight from the bush. That's where the English proverb "a bird in hand is worth two in the bush" came from. The proverb means that it is better to hold on to the thing that you already have, instead of taking the risk of going for something that may seem like a better offer, but may actually amount to nothing.

43. It Rained Cats and Dogs

In the 17th century, London was not a very sanitary place. Dead pets and waste from butcheries would be thrown among other things in heaps of garbage and left on the streets. When the rains were particularly heavy, these carcasses and garbage would be washed up in the flood which would end up in the River Fleet and other water bodies. In the wake of the storm, carcasses of cats and dogs could be spotted floating on the water or lying along the banks of the river, which gave the impression that they had somehow fallen along with the rain. Poets from that era, including one Jonathan Swift, often described this phenomenon in colorful terms, and that's how "it rained cats and dogs" came to mean it rained heavily.

44. A Shot in the Arm

At the start of the 20th century in America, it was common for people to inject themselves with drugs or vitamins in the upper arm. Back then, there were no strict regulations regarding medicines, narcotics, supplements, and hypodermic needles, so anyone could just buy such things or even get them from physicians or traders. People who shot themselves with substances, many of which are considered illegal today, often reported instantly feeling invigorated, stronger, or healthier. So, at that time, "a shot in the arm" was understood to mean an injection of a substance that would cause instant stimulation and give a person more energy or renewed enthusiasm. The phrase began to appear in newspaper reports, and with time, it started to be used metaphorically to mean a "stimulus." Today, we use the phrase to mean an addition that has an immediate positive effect on something.

45. To use a sledgehammer to crack a nut

In old English, sledges were large iron hammers that were mostly used by iron workers and miners. However, by the 15th century, the term had become so uncommon that people started to refer to sledges as sledgehammers. A few centuries later, in America in the 1850s, people would use small, regular hammers to crack tree nuts. The phrase "a hard nut to crack" came to mean a problem or puzzle that was hard to figure out. The implication here is that hard nuts are the exception and not the rule, as long as you have the right tool. In other words, nuts are relatively minor problems. It's based on this information that the phrase "using a sledgehammer to crack a nut" was coined to mean using disproportionate force or resources to overcome a fairly minor problem.

46. A Red Rag to a Bull

The phrase "to wave a red rag to a bull" means to deliberately provoke someone or something with the intention to cause an adverse or negative reaction. This phrase often evokes images of traditionally clad Spanish bullfighters, but that actually has nothing to do with its origin. Back in the early 17th century, "red rag" was a colloquial term for the tongue, so "waving the red rag" was a metaphor for "talking excessively." Later on, people discovered that they could use actual red rags to attract and trap birds such as pheasants and turkeys. There were also reports that the color red could be used to agitate snakes. After red rags started to be used in traditional bullfighting, the metaphor "red rag to a bull" started appearing in literary works. However, the truth is that bulls don't have the ability to see the color red, and any rag would do just fine. The choice of red is actually for the benefit of the spectators.

47. Till the cows come home

Back when Europe and Britain were mostly agrarian societies, herdsmen would take their cattle out to the pastures in the morning and bring them back home in the evening. The herdsmen quickly learned that it was almost impossible to predict how long it would take them to drive their cattle back home from the pastures because of how the cows behaved. While the other flock (the goats and sheep) would walk fast, the cows often walked lazily at slow and relaxed pace. They would stop to graze more if they spotted good patches of grass. They weren't in a hurry to get home, and they tested the herdsmen's patience. The timing of the herdsmen's arrival back home was completely at the mercy of the cows. That's how the expression "till the cows come home" came to mean for a long indefinite and unpredictable time.

48. To Go the Whole Nine Yards

During the Second World War, American combat planes were equipped with big machine guns that were used to fire incessantly at targets. To solve the problem of having to reload the machine guns frequently, the bullets for the gun were packed into heavy chains called gun belts that were twenty-seven feet, or nine yards, long. When the plane's crew encountered targets that were particularly challenging, they sometimes had to fire the entire gun belt at just one target. They started to refer to this as "giving the adversary the full nine yards." This became a common expression among service members and veterans after the war. In the 1960s, an athlete named Ralph Boston broke the world long jump record by jumping twenty-seven feet and half an inch. This was widely reported under the headline "Boston Goes the Whole Nine Yards!" It was after this report that the phrase gained wide usage. Today, "to go the whole nine yards" is commonly used to mean to go all the way or to take full measure.

49. Achilles heel

Achilles is one of the most well-known demigod heroes from Greek mythology. The story goes that when Achilles was born, there was a prophecy that he would die at a very young age. His mother, Thetis, wanting to save her child's life, took him to the river Styx, held him by one leg, and dipped him in the water. The river offered the little boy the power of invulnerability and he grew to be one of the greatest warriors who ever lived. The problem was that when his mother dipped him in the river, the small part of his heel that she held onto didn't come in contact with the magical water, so it remained weak. Achilles could only be killed by shooting an arrow into that heel. The expression "Achilles heel" was derived from this story. It means a small weakness or vulnerability in spite of overall strength, one that could lead to the downfall of someone or something.

50. To Spill the Beans

The phrase "to spill the beans," which means to divulge a secret either accidentally or maliciously, actually originates from an old Greek democratic tradition. The story goes that in ancient Greek, the legislature would vote on issues using beans. Each person would be handed a white bean and a dark bean. After a matter was tabled and discussed, a collector would go around with an opaque jar, and the legislators would each toss a dark or white bean into the jar. Many laws back then would only pass if the vote was unanimous. So if the collector would accidentally spill the jar of beans and it was revealed that there were dark beans among them, there would be no need to keep voting on that matter. By spilling the beans, the secret outcome of the vote would be revealed.

Did you know?

Stanford University has conducted clinical studies that show that people who experience auditory hallucinations, like schizophrenia, hear voices that are shaped by cultural influences. In Africa and India, voices are described to belong to family members or spirits, while in America, people describe voices as violent, torturous, and hateful yelling from strangers. This proves that culture shapes both the course and the outcome of psychosis. Psychiatrists now believe that the severity of psychosis can be reduced if patients are taught to perceive the voices as friendly instead of antagonistic.

According to recent scientific findings, the five tastes or senses that your tongue can recognize are sweet, sour, salty, bitter, and umami. Parmesan cheese is an example of umami. The flavor can also be found in anchovies, soy sauce, seared meats, among other foods. Adding MSG (monosodium glutamate) to food is an easy way to incorporate the umami flavor, but in the West, MSG is believed to be unhealthy.

In the Middle Ages, when bunny ears were put behind a man's head, it meant that his wife was cheating on him. The two fingers held up symbolized the horns of a stag, which had apparently lost its mate to a rival stag. Mischievous people would sneak up behind the man in question and flash the "cuckold's horns" symbol to insult him in front of onlookers. In the early days of photography, people would flash the bunny ears over their unwitting friends as a joke. Today, much of this has been forgotten and the bunny ears are mostly known as a symbol of peace.

51. Ace in the hole

In the game of poker, a card is said to be "in the hole" when it's hidden from view of the other players or spectators. A player can receive a card from the dealer, take a glimpse at it, and leave it lying face-down, saving if for use in a subsequent play. The other players are often left guessing what that card might be, or dreading that it might be an especially potent card. The ace is the most valuable card in the whole deck. So, if the card that the player has "in the hole," known in poker lingo as a "hole card," turns out to be an ace, it could give them the winning hand. That's why the American expression "ace in the hole" means information or some kind of resource that is held in reserve and can be used to give one a great advantage in a specific situation. The phrase "ace in the hole" was used in the context of poker since the 19th century, but it came to mainstream use after the 1951 movie "Ace in the Hole" was released. It was about a man who chose to delay saving someone just so he could benefit from reporting on the incident.

52. THE ACID TEST

Back in the 18th century, prospectors had a difficult time telling the difference between gold and other metals that looked similar. Some people wasted time and resources thinking they were mining gold, but it turned out to be base metals. Others bought specks of gold from shady sellers only to find out later that it was pyrite, commonly known as "fool's gold." There was a need for a quick and reliable way for both prospectors and traders to identify gold. Fortunately, in the latter half of the 18th century, someone figured out that nitric acid would dissolve most other metals at a faster rate than it could dissolve gold. A standard test was developed where the material in question would be scratched onto a touchstone, then acid would be added and the rate of dissolution would be observed. This became known as "the acid test" and it always gave accurate results. That's how the term "acid test" came to be used to mean a simple but sure test that gives incontestable results.

53. Abracadabra

"Abracadabra" is an explanation used by stage magicians and illusionists when performing tricks, and it's even sometimes used colloquially to imply that a certain outcome is magical. The term has been around in one form or another for millennia. The earliest known version of the term is the Aramaic expression "avra kadavra" which means "it will be created by my words." In ancient Rome, the word was used by roman sages and conjurers in various rituals. In medieval Europe, most people believed in magic, and the word "abracadabra" was used as an incantation to ward off evil bewitchment. If, for instance, someone believed that their illness was caused by witchcraft, a ritual would be performed where the word would be chanted repeatedly, with the last letter removed on each subsequent chant, with the last chant being just the letter "a." The idea was that the curse would get weaker as the word got shorter. The word was also written on charmed amulets that were sold by medicine men.

54. Hold a candle to something

For centuries, people learned skills and trades through apprenticeships. Master workers would find young men that showed promise in their craft, and they would let them work as their assistants while they learned the intricacies of their trade. Apprentices would carry out errands, hand over tools, or even prepare food for their masters. In the era before the advent of electricity, craftsmen who worked at night or in dark areas would require their apprentices to hold a candle or lamp for them to illuminate whatever they were working on. So, the phrase "to hold a candle for someone" came to mean to work under someone, probably as an apprentice. Apprenticeship was seen as a lowly position, but it still had a level of respectability to it because it meant that one had potential and could turn into a master in the future. There were people who were seen as completely lacking in potential, either because they were lazy or they lacked the smarts. The expression "can't hold a candle to someone" was coined back in the 17th century to describe such people. To date, we still use it to mean someone who compares so terribly to a known authority, that they wouldn't even be fit to hold a subordinate position to that authority.

55. Rub the wrong way

The phrase "to rub someone the wrong way" is commonly used today to mean "to irritate someone" or to act in a manner that annoys or angers someone. It actually dates back to the colonial era in America. Well-to-do families would construct opulent homes, complete with high-end wooden floors. The floorboards were made of expensive oak and they needed to be cleaned in a very careful manner. Sometimes, when the maids scrubbed the floors, they wouldn't follow the process outlined to them by their mistresses, and this would leave permanently, ugly marks on the floors. This would annoy the mistresses, and it would often invite serious punishment. The phrase "to rub the wrong way" started out in reference to wood floors, but over time, its origin was forgotten and it became purely metaphorical.

56. A BAKER'S DOZEN

A "dozen" means twelve, so why does a "baker's dozen" mean thirteen? Well, back in medieval England, bakers were small business owners who didn't have access to accurate measuring equipment. They just used their eyes and their years of experience to estimate the size and weight of the loaves they baked. The problem was that it was against the law for bakers and other traders to sell goods that were under the indicated weight. If a baker sold a dozen loaves, and they turned out to be short of the required weight, their reputation could be ruined, or worse yet, they could be fined or banned from their trade if the customer in question was influential. So, to protect themselves, when bakers sold a dozen loaves, they'd toss in an extra one, making a total of thirteen. This tradition stuck through the centuries, and even as accurate scales became available to bakers, they still kept giving their customers an extra loaf as an incentive to encourage loyalty.

57. Cut to the Chase

We often ask people to "cut to the chase," meaning that they should avoid wasting time with a lot of unnecessary details and quickly get to the point. This phrase originates from the early days of Hollywood. Back in the era of silent film, the dialogue scenes were considered really boring, and people were more interested in dramatic, action-packed scenes. Many old films, especially those in the comedy genre, often have elaborate chase scenes as part of their climax. It was common for audiences that had already seen a movie once to yell at the projectionist to fast forward the movie to the exciting scenes during subsequent screenings. When studio executives learned about this, they started discouraging directors and screenwriters from padding their films with too much unnecessary dialogue. During film edits, before they were released to the public, executives would watch the new movies, identify areas of lengthy, boring dialogue, and tell the filmmakers to "cut to the chase." The phrase started to appear on screenplays, and it became part of business lingo even outside Hollywood, before it gained mainstream use.

58. ABOVE BOARD

When we say that something is to be done "above board," we mean that it's to be done openly, and without any trickery or hidden intent. This phrase dates back to the 17th century when piracy was rampant in the high seas. Back then, the word "board" was synonymous with the word "deck," and "below board" meant "below deck." As pirate ships approached the vessels they were targeting, they would take down their distinctive flags and all the disheveled looking pirates would go below deck. That way, if the captain of the target ship were to look through his binoculars, there would be no clue that the approaching vessel was a pirate ship. Soon, ship crews learned that vessels that didn't seem to have any people "above board" were just pirate ships trying to trick or lull them into a false sense of security.

59. Wet blanket

For centuries, people have been using water-soaked blankets to put out fires. A wet blanket is both flexible and heavy, and it can cool most flammable materials and seal a given area, cutting out the supply of air that fans the flames. Starting in the 18th century, "fire" has been used figuratively to describe "the desire that burns inside a person" or "the spirit and drive in a person or a group." So, "putting out the fire" started to mean "discouraging or dampening a desire." From these ideas, the simile "like a wet blanket" emerged to describe people who had the tendency to discourage others from pursuing certain goals or desires. As time went by, that simile turned into a direct metaphor where "a wet blanket" took on the meaning a person or thing that speaks or acts to the effect of keeping other people from doing what they want or enjoying themselves.

60. Not for all the tea in China

Tea drinking originated in southwest China, and historical records of tea drinking date back to the 3rd century AD. Tea was first introduced to the West in the 16th century when Portuguese missionaries and merchants brought it back from China. By the 17th century, tea had become popular in Britain and its colonies, and there was robust tea trade between China and the West. Since Britain enjoyed such an abundant supply of tea from China, there was a sense in the British Isles that China had virtually unlimited fields of tea. This idea was reinforced further when Britain grew tired of China's tea monopoly and decided to introduce tea farming in India, its colony at the time. Because of this, people started using the phrase "not for all the tea in China" to mean "not for any price". They used the phrase to indicate that they were not willing to do something even if the potential upside was apparently unlimited.

Did you know?

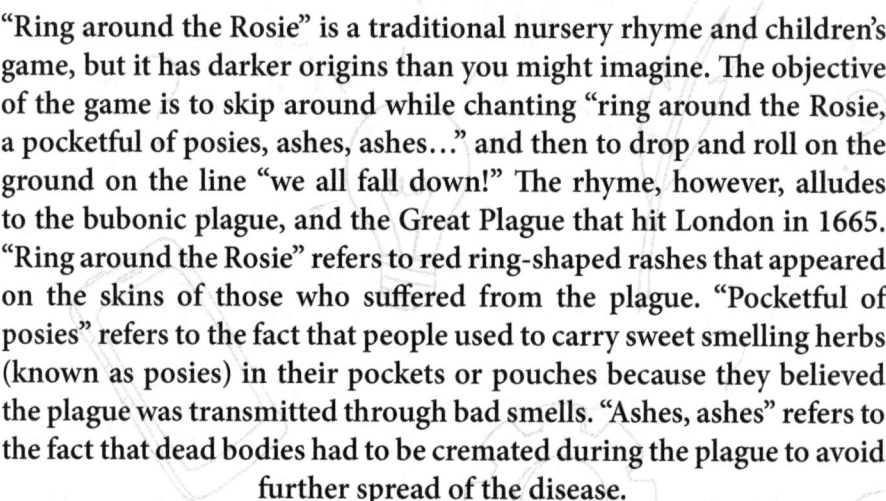

"Ring around the Rosie" is a traditional nursery rhyme and children's game, but it has darker origins than you might imagine. The objective of the game is to skip around while chanting "ring around the Rosie, a pocketful of posies, ashes, ashes…" and then to drop and roll on the ground on the line "we all fall down!" The rhyme, however, alludes to the bubonic plague, and the Great Plague that hit London in 1665. "Ring around the Rosie" refers to red ring-shaped rashes that appeared on the skins of those who suffered from the plague. "Pocketful of posies" refers to the fact that people used to carry sweet smelling herbs (known as posies) in their pockets or pouches because they believed the plague was transmitted through bad smells. "Ashes, ashes" refers to the fact that dead bodies had to be cremated during the plague to avoid further spread of the disease.

Minus forty degrees Fahrenheit and minus forty degrees Celsius are exactly the same temperatures. A physicist named Daniel Gabriel Fahrenheit devised the Fahrenheit scale using the coldest temperature that he could produce using brine as the zero point, and the temperature of the human body as one hundred. An astronomer named Anders Celsius used the freezing and boiling points of water as his zero point and one hundred when he developed the centigrade scale, which was later renamed to Celsius. These two scales ought to intersect at one temperature point, and it just happens to be minus forty degrees.

61. ALL AT SEA

Before navigation was nailed down to a science, there was always a risk when people set sail that they might never make it back to land. Before there were accurate navigational aids, even the most experienced ship crew could get lost. So if someone was "at sea" there was a great degree of uncertainty about his well being. People who went out to sea also came back with reports of feeling disoriented and having no sense of direction. Sometimes such people would experience a state of panic or discomfort known as sea sickness. That's how the expression "all at sea" came to mean feeling lost or confused.

62. Namby Pamby

When you say someone or something is "namby-pamby," it means that he or she is childish, weak, or excessively sentimental. This expression was coined as an insult to a British playwright and poet named Ambrose Philips back in the 18th century. Philips was hired to tutor George the First's grandchildren, an occupation that gave him some standing with the aristocracy. Because he wanted to be more accepted in those circles, he wrote sycophantic works praising the children of those aristocrats, often using language other writers considered tasteless. Other writers of his era hated and ridiculed his work, and they parodied it in a poem entitled *Namby-Pamby* in 1725. All writers started calling Phillip "Namby-Pamby," and by the end of the 18th century, the term was commonly used to critique all writing that seemed weak, fake, and ineffectual.

63. Beat around the bush

In medieval times, people would go bird hunting in groups. When they came across a bush that looked like there were fowls or quails nesting underneath, the members of the hunting team would surround it with outstretched nets in their arms. One or two members of the group would then literally beat the bush with sticks. If there were birds in the bush, they'd be startled, and they'd come flying out, right into the hunters' nets. This hunting method worked, but it was very inefficient. For instance, the hunters might have to beat dozens of bushes before they could find one that actually had birds in it. Sometimes they'd beat one bush only for the birds to come flying out of another bush nearby. That's how the expression "to beat about the bush" or "to beat around the bush" came to mean to talk or act in an evasive manner, or to deliberately avoid coming to the main point of a conversation.

64. To pass with flying colors

Before modern long distance communication technology was developed, ships had no way of sending messages back home to let their countries know how they were faring. So, when warships were engaged in battle at sea, the people on land wouldn't know if they had won or lost, until the ships sailed back. Similarly, ships that went on expeditions had to sail back to bring good or bad news. Explorers and navies at the time devised a simple way of letting people know whether they were victorious in battle or successful in their mission as soon as the ship could be spotted in the horizon. A successful or victorious ship would raise the country's flags high up on all its masts as they sailed towards the shore. People would gather by the sea a cheer as the ship came in. Ships that had faced defeat, on the other hand, would lower their flags, and the people onshore would brace for more details of the bad news. It's from this maritime tradition that the phrase "to pass with flying colors" emerged. Today, we use it to mean that one has passed a test or exam with exceptionally high scores.

65. As dead as a dodo

In the early 16th century, Portuguese explorers travelled to the island of Mauritius and came back with news about an odd, flightless bird known as a dodo. Over the next century and a half, more Portuguese and Dutch settlers moved into Mauritius, took over the land, and introduced domestic animals to the island. The dodo was big and slow, so it couldn't compete for food with chickens and other domestic animals, and this led to its extinction. The last reported sighting of a live dodo was in 1662, and by 1690, the bird was believed to be extinct. Following that, phrases like "as rare as a dodo" and "as extinct as a dodo" started to appear in works of literature and newspaper columns. It wasn't until 1865, when Lewis Carroll's *Alice's Adventures in Wonderland* featured a dodo character, that the simile "as dead as a dodo" came into popular use. We still use the phrase today to mean that someone is unequivocally dead, or something is no longer valid, effective, or interesting.

66. TO GET COLD FEET

Harsh weather has always been a major challenge in battlefields. In medieval Europe, when armies marched over long distances in the winter, by the time they got to the field of battle, a significant percentage of the infantry troops would be suffering from serious frostbite. Such soldiers were unable to fight because the nerves in their feet had been damaged by the cold. So, when the phrase "having cold feet" was first used, it meant "unable to fight because of frostbite." This phrase found common use across Europe, and in the 19th century, it appeared in works of literature in both English and German. The German novelist Fritz Reuter used "getting cold feet" to mean "losing one's nerves." The American novelist Stephen Crane used it to mean "to lose courage or enthusiasm." Today, we use the phrase to mean to back out of a serious commitment at the last minute or to be disheartened or to become timid, thereby losing your enthusiasm or courage.

67. As mad as a hatter

Between the 17th and 19th centuries, mercury was used to turn animal hair into felt, which was then used to make hats. Back then, people didn't understand the poisonous effects of mercury, so hat makers didn't take any safety precautions when handling the substance. Many hat makers, who were then referred to as "hatters," started exhibiting neurotoxic symptoms associated with mercury poisoning, including mood swings, aggressiveness, and many other antisocial behavior. In some extreme cases, these hatters would go into trembling fits. People observed that many hatters were literally going mad, but they had no way of understanding what caused the madness, so they named the condition "the Mad Hatter's Disease," a term that's still used in medical textbooks today. The phrase "mad as a hatter" started to appear in print in the early 19th century, and at the time it meant "annoyed." However, it was Lewis Carroll's *Alice's Adventures in Wonderland* that really brought the expression to mainstream use. Today "mad as a hatter" is used to mean completely mad or really crazy.

68. As happy as a clam

The phrase "as happy as a clam" is used to imply that someone is very happy and content. But why clams? Well, as it turns out, this phrase is a shortened version of a longer simile that originated from the American Northeast. Fishermen and mariners had noticed that most sea predators would swim away at high tide, and clams would then come out and swim around carefree without being attacked. So, they coined the phrase "as happy as a clam at high tide." The phrase was so widely used in the region, that in the early 19th century, it was no longer necessary to say it in its entirety, as people were already familiar with it. However, by the late 20th and early 21st centuries, people had forgotten the root of the phrase, and they just started assuming it had something to do with the "smile shape" of the bivalve mollusk.

69. AS EASY AS PIE

The idiom "as easy as pie" has a complicated origin that may have nothing to do with pie at all. The phrase originated in Australia in the 1920s from the term "pie at" or "pie on" which meant "to be very good at something." The word "pie" in this context comes from the word "pai" which is the Maori term for "good." This meaning of the word pie is evident in some works of literature that predate the phrase. For example, Mark Twain used "pie" to mean "generally pleasant and accommodating." The first time the two meanings of pie appeared to merge was in a publication where the phrase "like eating pie" was used to refer to experiences that were generally pleasant. After that, "as easy as pie" started to be used to mean "very easy." It should be noted that the ease has to do with eating pie, not making pie. Making pie is actually a fairly complicated process.

70. Dead ringer

"A dead ringer" means "an exact duplicate" of someone or something. The phrase is used to refer to things that one cannot tell apart just by looking. To understand the origin of the phrase, we must first understand what the words "dead" and "ringer" mean in this context. Here, "dead" has the same meaning that it does in the phrase "dead on," which means "absolute and exact." It was originally used in marksmanship to mean that a shot was exactly on target. The term "ringer" comes from an old slang phrase "to ring" which meant "to switch, exchange, or substitute." The phrase "dead ringer" was first used in horse racing in the US when unscrupulous horse owners would switch two horses that looked exactly the same in order to defraud bookies, buyers, and punters. For instance, a slow horse with longshot odds could be switched with a faster one that resembled it, and the owner would bet and win big if the fake horse performed well.

Did You Know?

On January 13, 1996, nine-year-old Amber Hagerman was kidnapped and murdered, and the killer was never found. The Amber Alert that is put out when a child goes missing actually came about after this sad event. It alerts local broadcasters and law enforcement to come together to get information out quickly following a child's abduction. It's known nationwide as an Amber Alert, which stands for "America's Missing Broadcast Emergency Response."

"Mayday" is a term used internationally as a distress signal. It comes from the French "venez m'aider," which translates to "come help me." The term was coined in the 1920s by a radio officer named Frederick Stanley who worked in a London airport. The officer was asked to create an emergency signal that could easily be understood by all pilots and airport personnel. Because much of the air traffic at the airport was between London and Paris, the officer picked "Mayday" because it would be immediately recognizable to French speakers.

The title "Mrs." has an "r" in it because the abbreviation comes from mistress, not missus. Mistress is the female version of the word "master," which is in fact the real origin of the abbreviation "Mr." Today, in the English speaking world, the word "mister" is more commonly used than the word "master," but since "mister" has an "r" the abbreviation doesn't cause confusion. The word mistress has negative connotations today, but back in the 18th century, it was an honorific title for a wealthy woman who had servants.

71. As the crow flies

The phrase "as the crow flies" means in a direct or straight line, without any turns or detours as with following a normal road. This phrase clearly alludes to the ability of crows and other birds to fly directly from point A to point B, as opposed to how humans are forced to work their way around the terrain and other features or follow an established path. The reason "the crow" (and not any other bird) is specifically used in the expression, has to do with a very old method of navigation. Before there were reliable compasses, sailors would keep crows in cages on their ships. If they were lost, they would release one crow, watch the direction in which it chose to fly, then follow it in the hopes that it would lead them back to land. The phrase "straight as the crow flies" was used by Charles Dickens in *Oliver Twist*, and that's what made the expression popular.

72. To give something a wide berth

The phrase "to give a wide berth" to someone or something means "to stay a good distance away" from that person or thing. The phrase originates from the nautical tradition of the 17th century. The word "berth" refers to the place on a dock or wharf that's allotted to a specific ship. Early spellings of "berth" indicate that the word is closely related to "birth" which means "bearing of offspring." So, "berth" was originally seen as a place where a ship could "bear off" into the sea. However, with time, "berth" generally came to refer to "space between ships," whether those ships were docked or were out at sea. That's when sailors started to use the phrase "give wide berth" to mean "stay out of the way" of other ships. The phrase later gained wider figurative use, mostly in contexts where people were being warned to stay away from things that could potentially cause them harm.

73. As thick as thieves

Back in the 18th century, the word "thick" was sometimes used to mean "closely allied with." So, when two or more people were described as "thick," it often meant that they had a close, almost impenetrable relationship that made others feel excluded. In the same era in England, groups that were in the fringes of society often used secret words to communicate and to protect their identities. These included thieves, poachers, homosexuals, gypsies, and many other secret societies that were considered illegal or shunned by society. Gangs of thieves were particularly known for their use of virtually incomprehensible words, including back slang (which were words pronounced backwards). The simile "as thick as thieves" emerged because of their use of secretive and conspiratorial language that made no sense to others.

74. At loggerheads

In medieval England, people would fasten a thick block of timber to a horse's leg to keep it from running away while the owner wasn't paying attention. This block of wood was known as a "logger," so "logger-head" literally meant "block-head" back then. Based on that, calling someone a "logger-head" meant that he was a foolish or stupid person or a dunce. This use of the word even appears in Shakespeare's work. In the 17th century, a long rod with a metal ball welded to one end was used as a tool in shipbuilding, and domestically to melt frozen ice. This tool was kept near the fireplace in some homes, and it became known as a "loggerhead." Sometimes, when people would get into heated disagreements or fights while indoors, they would pick up the loggerheads and start swinging them at each other. That's how the expression "to be at loggerheads with someone" came to mean to be in a dispute, a disagreement or a quarrel with someone.

75. The whole shebang

We use the phrase "the whole shebang" today to mean "the whole thing" or "all of it." The word "shebang" originates from the Confederacy during the American Civil War. The Confederate army would often set up camp in haste, and they'd fail to come up with properly constructed tents or structures. They borrowed the word "shebang" from the original Irish word "shebeen" which basically means "rustic or makeshift dwelling," which perfectly described most of the structures in their camps. Because of the poor quality of all the structures, the term "shebang" was used to refer to everything from tents, cabins, shops, huts, armories, and engine houses. The term spread across America after the war, and it was used to describe living quarters such as student dormitories that were seen as low quality. Towards the end of the 19th century, there were many expressions used in different parts of America that started with "the whole," including the whole enchilada" and "the whole nine yards." "The whole shebang" emerged as one such phrase. The word "shebang" actually had nothing to do with "wholeness," it was just used because it made a catchy phrase. The phrase stuck around, and today its meaning is universally understood, even though most people have no idea what "shebang" means.

76. Young Turks

The term "Young Turk" is used mostly in a political context to refer to a young person who is full of new, seemingly radical ideas, and is perceived by those that have been around longer to be impatient in his or her push for change. The term comes from a real Turkish political movement from the early 20th century that was known as Young Turks. This movement pushed for a constitutional democracy to be set up in place of the absolute monarchy that reigned over the Ottoman Empire at the time. The Young Turks led a revolution against the Sultan and were successful in ushering in a multi-party democracy in the country. In the decades following the revolution, establishment politicians both in the US and the UK started referring to younger politicians who stood up against weak leadership as "Young Turks" and that's how the term gained its figurative use.

77. Bells and whistles

Before we had sirens and public address systems, those who wanted to draw attention to themselves in public spaces would ring bells and blow whistles. Bells and whistles were used by traders in open markets, members of religious groups such as the Salvation Army, circuses, theaters and other performers parading through towns to announce their arrival, government announcers, among others. Even as industrialization advanced, bells and whistles were used by locomotives, fire engines, and factories to announce shift changes. Because of all this, "bells and whistles" became a euphemism for things that are meant to grab your attention. This figurative use of the phrase was common from the 18th to the early 20th century. However, with time, as people's expectations of technological advancement went higher, the meaning of "bells and whistles" evolved, and the phrase was increasingly used to refer to products such as cars (and later computers) which came with a full array of extra features. That's why the phrase now means attractive additional fittings or features.

78. Below the belt

The phrase "to hit someone below the belt," which means to use an underhanded or unfair tactic to win against someone, originates from 18th century boxing rules. The sport of boxing used to be savage and arbitrary, until 1743 when a London boxer named Jack Broughton was hired to outline clear rules that everyone was to follow. He wrote "The London Prize Ring Rules," in which he stated that competitors should not hit their adversaries when they were down, on their knees, grab them by the shorts, or hit them in "any part below the waist." Although these boxing rules were coined in Britain, the words "below the belt" were first used in an American newspaper in an article that paraphrased the official rules. Even though boxers don't actually wear belts while in the ring, it's this American version of the phrase that eventually gained widespread figurative usage.

79. Have your work cut out for you

Tailoring and garment making has existed as a vocation for the entirety of human history. For centuries, tailors have had a very systematic way of making batches of garments. First, they would measure everything out of the required fabric and cut out all the pieces that they needed. This was the easy part of the job. After everything was cut and properly organized, the tailors would start the tedious and painstaking process of sewing the garments, one by one, until the whole batch was finished. That's the origin of the phrase "to have your work cut out for you." The phrase originally meant "to be faced with a very large amount of well-defined work." It has been appearing in print as far back as the 16th century. However, as technology advanced over the centuries, the meaning of the phrase changed, and now "having your work cut out for you" refers less to the volume or amount of the work and more to the complexity or difficulty of the work.

80. Basket case

After the First World War, many American veterans came back home with serious injuries. Some had lost their limbs while others had lost their eyes or were badly disfigured as a result of fire or chemical burns. Most people knew someone who had been crippled during the war. Because of the horrific nature of some of the injuries that the vets suffered, exaggerated accounts of war stories started to emerge. One such story was a popular urban legend from the time, which claimed that some soldiers had lost all four limbs and were completely incapable of doing anything for themselves, so they had to be carried everywhere in a "large basket." These "limbless veterans" were referred to as "basket cases." There are actually no official records of such soldiers, but people at the time often claimed to "know somebody who knows somebody" who had lost both hands and both legs. In the latter half of the 20th century, the term "basket case" came to refer to a person or thing that's failing and is unable to function properly. It was mostly used to refer to people who had mental issues or breakdown, but in recent years, it's more often used to denounce schemes and organizations that are failing.

Did you know?

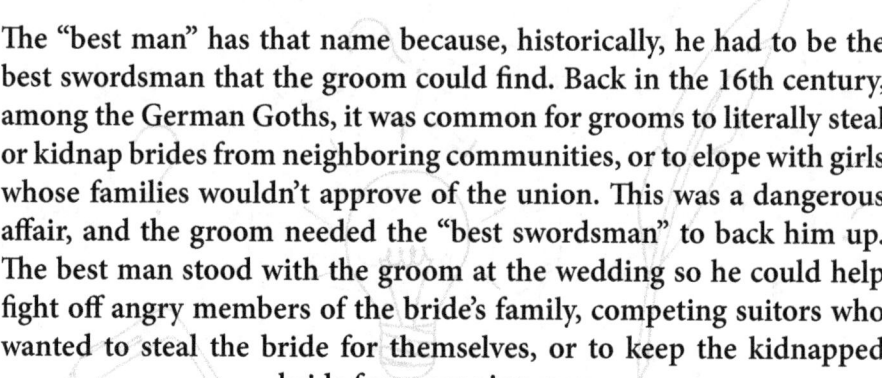

The "best man" has that name because, historically, he had to be the best swordsman that the groom could find. Back in the 16th century, among the German Goths, it was common for grooms to literally steal or kidnap brides from neighboring communities, or to elope with girls whose families wouldn't approve of the union. This was a dangerous affair, and the groom needed the "best swordsman" to back him up. The best man stood with the groom at the wedding so he could help fight off angry members of the bride's family, competing suitors who wanted to steal the bride for themselves, or to keep the kidnapped bride from running away.

The term "freelancer" comes from the medieval era, when warriors were not under the oath of any lord, hence making them a freelancer. The term "lance" refers to a long spear with a steel tip which knights carried with them when they rode their horses. A "lancer" is anyone who carries or uses a lance. Freelancers were essentially medieval mercenaries who fought for the king or lord that paid the most.

Originally, the word outlaw meant "outside the protection of the law." In other words, you could rob or kill an outlaw without having legal consequences. Before modern legal systems were enacted in Europe, a person who was considered a criminal would be declared an outlaw, meaning that they would lose all rights accorded to other good citizens. This meant that people were permitted to do anything to the outlaws, including persecuting or killing them.

81. Sleep tight

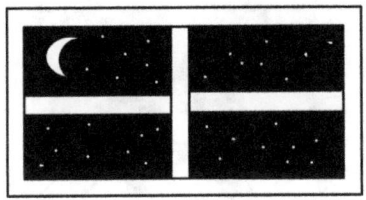

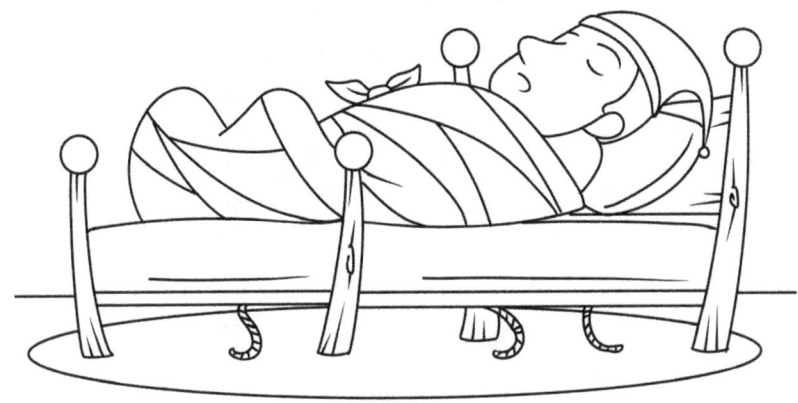

Back in the 19th and 20th centuries, some beds were made in a different way than they are today. Ropes were woven to bed frames to make flat mesh surfaces on which the mattresses were to be placed. After someone had slept on such a bed for a while, the ropes would start to sag, and that made for an uncomfortable night's sleep. The ropes therefore had to be regularly tightened to ensure that the mattress was always placed on a taut and firm surface. That's where the nighttime pleasantry "sleep tight" comes from. While it just means "have a good night's sleep" today, back then, it expressed a wish that one's bed was adequately tight to facilitate a restful night. Also, at the time, mattresses were just large bags stuffed with things like feathers, straw or grass; materials that attracted lots of bedbugs. That's why the phrase "sleep tight" is often followed with "don't let the bedbugs bite."

82. Put a sock in it

The First World War featured a long and brutal technique known as trench warfare, a practice where soldiers would hide or seek shelter in dugout trenches. Enemy soldiers would fire machine guns and throw hand grenades aimlessly into the other side's trenches, hoping to hit soldiers that they couldn't see. If a soldier was hit and injured by sheer luck, he would start screaming in pain. His friends, fearing that the noise would give away their position in the trenches, would take a sock and shove it into the injured soldier's mouth to muffle the sound. So to "put a sock" in someone's mouth was a literal action taken by soldiers out of necessity. Immediately after the war, around 1919, the expression "put a sock in it" was officially defined as a British slang term that meant leave off talking, shouting or singing. Today, the phrase is considered a rude way of asking or telling someone to shut up.

83. Goody two shoes

The phrase "goody two-shoes" is commonly used to criticize or disparage people who are perceived as "overly virtuous," either because they are too shy for their own good, too smug and judgmental, excessively sentimental, or their general manner makes others feel less moral. The phrase comes from a popular 18th century children's story called "The History of Little Goody Two-Shoes." The titular "little goody two-shoes" is an orphan girl named Margery Meanwell who starts out in a life filled with poverty, tragedy and despair, but grows up to lead a fulfilling, married life because of her virtuous nature. In a subplot of the story, Margery is so poor that she only owns a single shoe, but a well-meaning clergyman buys her a second shoe to match, so the little girl runs around and joyfully tells everyone that she now owns "two shoes." The word "goody" was originally short for "goodwife" which referred to poor, married women. Today, "goody" is generally understood to mean someone that's well-behaved or dutiful.

84. Crocodile tears

Centuries ago, people used to believe that crocodiles shed tears while consuming their prey. This belief was later proven to be incorrect, and scholars theorized that people might have observed crocodiles (which live in bodies of water), dripping with water near the eyes, and assumed that they were tears. Crocodiles do in fact have tear ducts but these are used to moisten the eyes when the creature has been out of water for a long period of time. The phrase "crocodile tears" actually exists in almost every European language because it was first coined back when most people in the region spoke Latin. It means false, superficial, or insincere display of emotions. It's used to describe displays of grief that are hypocritical or meant for one's own personal benefit.

85. Ball and chain

A ball and chain is a crude device that was historically locked onto prisoners' legs to physically restrain them. It was mostly used in the British Empire and its colonies (including America) between the 17th and 20th centuries. The chains were like ordinary shackles, but they were welded onto a heavy metal ball, which either made it impossible for the prisoner to move, or it slowed the prisoner down if he tried to escape. In its earlier figurative use, "ball and chain" used to mean "something that keeps one from doing what he wants." However, as times changed and women started to have more of a say in society, men who didn't particularly like their wives pushing for decisions that limited their ability to do whatever they wanted, started referring to their wives by the term "ball and chain." The term is still used colloquially to mean "wife."

86. In the Limelight

The word "lime" refers not just to the small citrus fruit, but also to a chemical compound known as calcium oxide, which is often called "quicklime." In the early 19th century, an inventor called Goldsworthy Gurney invented a lighting technique where he heated calcium oxide in a flame generated from burning hydrogen and oxygen. The product was an intense white light that was named "limelight." Limelight was first used in long distance surveying until, in 1837, when it was first used to light up a theater stage in Covent Garden in London. For the remainder of the 19th century, theaters all over the world started using the limelight in the form of a concentrated spotlight beam to focus on specific actors or zones on stage, and to create sunlight, moonlight, and other special effects. When the limelight was shone on an actor, it was a way of directing the audience's attention towards that person. That's how the phrase "to be in the limelight" came to mean to be at the center of people's attention.

87. Bail out

The phrases "to bail out" and "to bale out" have the same meaning, but interestingly, they have different origins. The word "bail" comes from the French word "baillier" which means bucket. The phrase "to bail out" originates from seafaring. When boats or ships were damaged and water started to leak in, the crew would frantically fetch the water in bucket loads and dump it overboard. This was called "bailing out the water." The word "bale" means "a large bundle bound for transportation or storage," as in "a bale of hay." The phrase "to bale out" originates from the early days of aviation when trapdoors would be used to offload heavy cargo midflight to keep the plane from crashing. This phrase took another meaning during the First World War when aviators had to jump off of damaged planes. Today, "bale out" and "bail out" both mean to stop doing something or stop participating in an endeavor.

88. Show your true colors

Back when piracy plagued the high seas, pirate ships would often fly flags or ensigns that belonged to particular countries or merchant companies when approaching their target ships. The crew on the target ship would be fooled into thinking that the approaching vessel belonged to a legitimate company or friendly country, and they wouldn't take evasive action or prepare for an attack. However, as the pirate ship came within close range of the target ship, it would lower the fake flags and raise its dreadful skull and crossbones flag, throwing the unsuspecting crew of the target ship into a state of panic and confusion. So, the pirate ship would start by flying "false colors" and, when the target was vulnerable, it revealed its "true colors." That's the origin of the phrase "to show your true colors" which means to shed all pretenses and to show what you are really like or to reveal one's character or nature.

89. The walls have ears

Royals and rulers have always had an obsession with knowing what people say about them behind their backs, so that they would figure out who they could or couldn't trust. In ancient Greece, about 400 BC, Dionysius, the ruler of Syracuse, was believed to have a gigantic ear-shaped underground chamber in his palace built specifically to listen to other people's conversations. This was more likely a myth or an exaggeration, but it had the effect of making the people in the court afraid of Dionysius. Later, in the 16th century, the Louvre Palace in Paris was constructed with a network of listening tubes targeting specific rooms. Because of this acoustic ingenuity, what was said in one room could be clearly heard in other secret rooms. This system was used by the ever-suspicious Queen Catherine de' Medici to spy on members of the palace court, so it was common for them to warn visiting dignitaries that "the walls have ears." That's how the proverb "walls have ears" came to be used as general advice to warn people about speaking too freely as someone might be eavesdropping, the literal meaning behind the "walls have ears."

90. Push the Envelope

We use the expression "to push the envelope" to mean an attempt to go beyond the current performance limits of a person or a thing or to continually innovate and challenge commonly accepted boundaries or limitations. The word "envelope," as used in this phrase, actually has nothing to do with the paper pocket that we use to mail letters. Here, the word refers to the mathematical envelope which is a technical term that means "the locus of ultimate intersections of consecutive curves." This concept is more easily understood if you consider the verb "to envelop" which can mean "to cover" or in a more mathematical sense, "to limit." The term "flight envelope" was used in aviation back in the 1940s to describe the upper and lower limits within which an aircraft can fly safely. These limits applied to factors such as speed, altitude, windiness, engine power, and maneuverability of the aircraft. Pilots, engineers, and researchers were always testing these limits to figure out how to make better planes or to improve training standards. Aviation insiders of that era started to refer to this practice as "pushing the envelope."

Did you know?

The red, white and blue colored stripes on the barber shop pole are actually a vestige from an era when barbershops were used for bloodletting. Bloodletting was a medical procedure from the Middle Ages which involved cutting one's veins open and letting blood drain away in the hopes of curing a wide variety of maladies. The procedure was originally performed by monks, but after the church stopped them, people had to turn to barbers. Barber shops were essentially outpatient clinics – they used to cut hair, do some bloodletting, set broken bones, and pull bad teeth. The red color on the barber pole represents the blood, while the white color represents bandages. The pole itself represents a special stick that people would hold onto during the bloodletting procedure. Later, in America, after much of the bloodletting tradition was forgotten, the blue stripe was added to the barber shop pole to match the American flag.

The New Year was celebrated between March 25 and April 1 by the French when the Julian calendar was still in use. However, in 1564, after the introduction of the new Gregorian calendar, the festivity was moved to January 1. While most people quickly adapted the new calendar because it was proposed by the church, some people resisted the change, and they subsequently became victims of elaborate jokes, hoaxes, and pranks. These people were invited to New Year's parties on the 1st of April only to show up and find that there was no party. They were also derided and referred to as "the April fools." That's how we ended up celebrating April Fools' Day on April 1st.

91. Badger to death

Centuries ago, before animal brutality was considered taboo in England, people would pit all sorts of animals against each other in fights in what was considered a spectator sport at the time. One such sport, known then as "badger-baiting," involved pitting badgers against dogs. Badgers are nocturnal burrowing mammals that are far more ferocious than one might assume. They were usually smaller than the dog that they went up against, but once they felt cornered by the dog, they would fight tenaciously, sometimes biting chunks of flesh off the dog. People gathered around, cheering and waging bets on the animals as they tore each other apart. The game would only stop when one of the animals was dead. More often than not, it was the badger that ended up dead. That was the origin of the English phrase "to badger someone to death," which we use today to mean to harass or to persecute someone.

92. Saved by the bell

In boxing, when one of the fighters is knocked to the ground, he has to get up before the referee gets to the count of ten, or his opponent wins the match. There is another rule that each round in the match is strictly timed, and when the clock runs out, a bell is rung, the fight stops instantly, and that specific round is over. These two rules would sometimes come into collision. Sometimes, a fighter would be knocked down and the referee would start the count, only for the bell to ring marking the end of the round, before the referee got to ten. In this case, the match would continue. It was said that the boxer on the ground was "saved by the bell" because he would likely have lost had the bell not rung at that opportune moment. That's why the phrase "saved by the bell" came to mean to escape a catastrophic or otherwise undesired outcome because of a last-minute intervention.

93. Armed to the teeth

Back in the 17th century, guns (particularly those used by pirates) were rudimentary compared to firearms today, they could only fire one shot before they needed to be reloaded. This meant that the pirates roaming the high seas at the time needed to carry as many guns with them as possible, even as they swung around on ropes trying to get onto the ships they were trying to loot. The pirates would stuff weapons in all pockets, in their boots, on holsters around their waists, on straps around their chests, on their hands, and when they ran out of ways to carry more weapons, they would hold an extra knife or sword between their teeth. That's where the phrase "armed to the teeth" comes from. The phrase is still used to mean "carrying many weapons," but in a more figurative sense, it means to be overly well equipped for something.

94. To go haywire

"Haywire" was originally a special kind of light wire that was sold to farmers in large spools, and was used to tie up huge rolls or bales of hay. However, in the 1900s, some loggers started using hay wire to repair their logging equipment. This practice was greatly discouraged by the authorities at the time, because while the logging equipment could still be used, it posed serious safety issues to those who used it because haywire would often snap off from the equipment at crucial moments, and some loggers were killed in the process. The US Forest Bureau published a report warning loggers not to join the "haywire outfit." The term "haywire outfit" became a contemptuous term for loggers who used hay wire to repair their equipment. As more cases of accidents were reported as a result of broken "haywire" in the logging industry, the phrase "to go haywire" was coined with the meaning "to go awry" or "to get out of control." Today, "go haywire" means go very wrong or go crazy, like in the case of an emotional outburst.

95. Barking up the Wrong Tree

In the early 19th century, people used to go hunting with packs of hounds. The dogs would spot the prey, chase it down until they caught it, and pin it down until the hunters caught up. However, some types of game animals, such as squirrels and wild rabbits, had the ability to run off and scurry up a tree. Since most dogs are unable to climb a tree in pursuit of prey, the only thing that they could do was run up to the tree in question, stand there, and bark continuously until the hunters arrived. Sometimes, the hunters would find the prey hiding in the branches of the tree and they would shoot it down. However in other cases, unbeknownst to the hunting dogs, the prey would jump from the branches of that tree to the next and so on until it vanished. When the hunters caught up and found the dog barking at the tree, they'd search the branches, only to find no prey. In such cases, the dogs were said to be "barking up the wrong tree." The phrase came to be used metaphorically to mean that one was pursuing a misguided or mistaken course of action or line of thought.

96. Hear something through the grapevine

After Samuel Morse invented the telegraph in 1844, there was a lot of public fascination about this new form of communication in the years that followed. People couldn't help comparing telegraph communication with the one form of communication that was most prevalent at the time – word of mouth. People observed that the telegraph wires resembled the vines and tendrils of grape plants in terms of thickness, but unlike the grapevines that were messy and twisted, the telegraph lines were very straight. Building on these comparisons, people started to jokingly refer to word of mouth communication as "the grapevine telegraph." So, instead of saying "I heard a rumor" or "I heard it through gossip," people would say "I heard it through the grapevine." Even as other means of communication took over and people forgot about the telegraph, the term "grapevine" stuck around, and today we still use it to mean "gossip."

97. Hands down

In horse racing, to get the horses to run faster, the jockeys usually pull hard on the reins that are roped around the horse's head. In doing so, the jockey has to position his hands forward. If the jockey lets go or loosens the tightness of the reins, the horse will likely slow down, switch to a trot, or come to a stop. In the 19th century, it was observed on occasion that when one horse was much faster than its competitors, and had left such a large distance between itself and the rest of the pack, the horse would still be guaranteed to win the race even if the jockey loosened his grip on the reins. Sometimes, if a jockey was totally sure that his horse was going to win no matter what, he would completely let go of the reins, and put his hands down, as a sign of hubris. In such cases, it would be reported that the horse and jockey had "won hands down." That's the origin of the expression "to win hands down" which means to win very easily, or with little effort.

98. Run of the Mill

The word "mill" originally referred to a wide variety of buildings that were equipped with machines which were used to grind wheat and other grains into flour. As new machines were invented, some of them were considered specialized mills (e.g. windmill and sawmill). When the textile processing machine was invented, it too was referred to as "the textile mill," or just "the mill." The textile mill was used to generate yards of fabric. This fabric was named "run of the mill" because it had just come straight out of the textile milling machine. It would then be taken to other machines where it would be cut, graded for quality, or dyed into different colors. There was no way of knowing the quality of the "run of the mill" fabric until it had undergone further processing. So, the phrase "run of the mill" took on the meaning "product of undefined quality." From there, the phrase gained wide usage, and it's now used to refer to things that are ordinary, average, or basic, and are not outstanding in any way (in terms of rarity or quality).

99. Break a Leg

In theater and other performing arts we say "break a leg" to wish performers good luck as they go on stage. This phrase originated in the Elizabethan era when theater was the prime art form. At the time, many performers were superstitious. They believed that wishing someone "good luck" would jinx them and result in bad luck. At first, people would avoid expressing any wish altogether. In the same era, the audiences would often bang their chairs on the floor instead of applauding. The more they liked the performance, the more they banged the chairs, and that would often result in someone breaking the leg off a chair or two. Soon, someone figured out a way to express a wish that sounded negative, but really had a positive meaning that only theater insiders would know. Performers started telling each other "I hope you break a leg" which sounded like it meant "I hope you get injured while performing" to avoid jinxing the performer, but both parties knew that it meant "I hope your performance is so well received that an audience member breaks a leg off a chair."

100. Get on a Soapbox

The expression "to get on one's soapbox" means to share one's opinions in a heartfelt, forceful, unrehearsed, and impromptu manner, more often to the annoyance of those with different views. The word originally had a literal meaning. Back in the day, before carton boxes and paper bags were invented, most goods were transported inside wooden crates, so it was common to find these crates lying around in markets, train stations, and other public areas. Crates with the word "SOAP" written on them were particularly easy to spot, so people started calling all wooden crates "soapboxes." When people such as striking workers and rights groups members held impromptu public meetings, someone would find a wooden crate and set it as a makeshift platform for whoever was speaking.

101. Honeymoon

Back in the 5th century, many cultures in the world, including Scandinavians, used the cycles of the moon to make the date of the calendar. "One moon" was equivalent to "one month." Scandinavians also commonly consumed mead, which was a traditional alcoholic brew made from fermented honey. Scandinavians believed that mead had an aphrodisiac effect, and it also increased fertility, so it was a requirement for all newly married couples to consume mead every single day for the first month of their marriage. Thus, the first month of marriage in Scandinavian tradition, was known as "the honey-moon." The term was adapted into many European languages over the centuries and it has had both negative and positive connotations over the years. For instance, in England in the 16th century, "honeymoon" which referred to the first month of marriage, was seen as a grace period for the newlyweds before the love wanes and the troubles kick in. Today, the word honeymoon itself is considered positive, but phrases such as "the honeymoon is over" imply that difficult times are around the corner.

Did you know?

One of the inventors of the Taser, John H. Jack Cover, named it after his literary hero Tom Swift. The word is actually an acronym for Thomas A. Swift's Electric Rifle. Cover just added the "A" to Tom Swift's name. He came up with the idea sometime in the late 1960s when he read an article about a man who accidentally walked into an electric fence and the shock made him unable to move for a few minutes. He created the Taser to help law enforcement officers stop the rampant cases of airplane hijackings.

The term "CAPTCHA" means Completely Automated Public Turing Test to Tell Computers and Humans Apart. CAPTCHAs are sometimes called "Reverse Turing Tests" because while traditional Turing Tests are administered by humans to a computer, CAPTCHAs are administered by a computer to a human.

Book two

1. All roads lead to Rome

"All roads lead to Rome" is a proverb that means that whatever methods you choose to do something, you will reach the same outcome in the end. It refers to something that is inevitable. This expression comes from the times of the Roman Empire when their roads were built so that they would diverge from the capitol resembling a wheel with Rome at its center. This analogy was already common in the 12th century. Its first printed use comes from the theologian and poet Alain de Lille that stated, "A thousand roads lead men forever to Rome."

2. Mark my words

"Mark my words" is an expression that is used to tell someone to pay attention to and remember what the speaker is saying. We apply this expression to alert someone that what we are about to say is important. On the other hand, "mark my words" often comes before a negative prediction that we are trying to emphasize. For example, we can say: "Mark my words, this will not end well!" This phrase can be found in the 1535 translation of *The Book of Isaiah*. It was meant to describe something ominous or dark that was going to happen.

3. Paddle your own canoe

When you "paddle your own canoe," that means that you are self-sufficient and independent. There are several origin sources found for this idiom. One source points out that the first mention of this phrase appears in *The Selangor Journal: Jottings Past and Present*, from 1807, which described the lack of cooperation between the coffee planters in Malaysia, stating that instead of working together, each planter "paddles their own canoe." Other sources single out the 1844 book *The Settlers in Canada*, written by Frederick Marryat, as the first known use of this expression.

4. Make a mountain out of a molehill

A person who "makes a mountain out of a molehill" is someone who greatly over-reacts when there is a minor problem or exaggerates when describing a problematic situation, making it look much worse than it is. The mountain represents something large, while a molehill, a tiny lump of dirt made by the digging of a mole, represents something much smaller. We use this idiom to describe or respond to someone falsely presenting their problems as great or unbearable and even to scold them for it. The idiom is found in Nicholas Udall's translation of *The first tome or volume of the Paraphrase of Erasmus upon the New Testamente* (1548).

5. IN A PICKLE

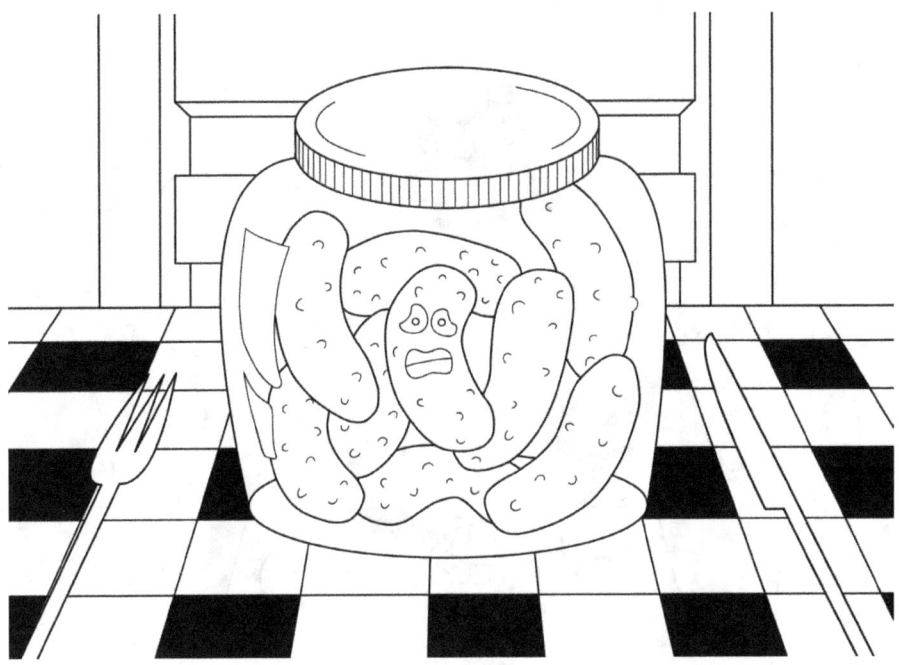

If you're "in a pickle," you're in a difficult position or you have a quandary that isn't easily solved. In the 16th century, the Dutch people had a phrase that translated to "sitting in a pickle" which they used to mean that someone was drunk. Another early usage of "in a pickle" was in Shakespeare's *The Tempest* when the character Alonso asks, "How camest thou in this pickle?" and Trinculo answers, "I have been in such a pickle since I saw you last that, I fear me, will never out of my bones…" which also translated to being drunk. While the origin of the phrase is meant to refer to drunk people, it has since adapted to mean someone is in a tough situation.

6. NO DICE

This phrase is commonly used to refuse someone's proposal or request, or suggests that there's no chance that something will happen. We can translate this expression as "no chance" and use it if we want to brush off or decline someone's unrealistic suggestion. The phrase first originated in America in the 20th century. Because gambling was illegal in many states at the time, gamblers caught in the act would take their dice and hide or swallow them in order to avoid being charged by the authorities. If the court found "no dice" in their possession, they couldn't make a case against them.

7. Harp on

To "harp on" something means to talk about something continuously or repeatedly in an irritating way. We use this idiom to describe someone's bothersome way of talking, lecturing, complaining, requesting something, or just constantly repeating a topic. The meaning of this expression is connected to the action of continually playing the harp on the same string, meaning "to play the same note over and over." The phrase was used by Shakespeare in several of his plays. In *Richard III*, the character of King Richard uses a variation of the phrase in his line, "Harp not on that string, madam; that is past." In Hamlet, the character of Polonius speaks to the audience saying, "How say you by that? Still harping on my daughter."

8. In cold blood

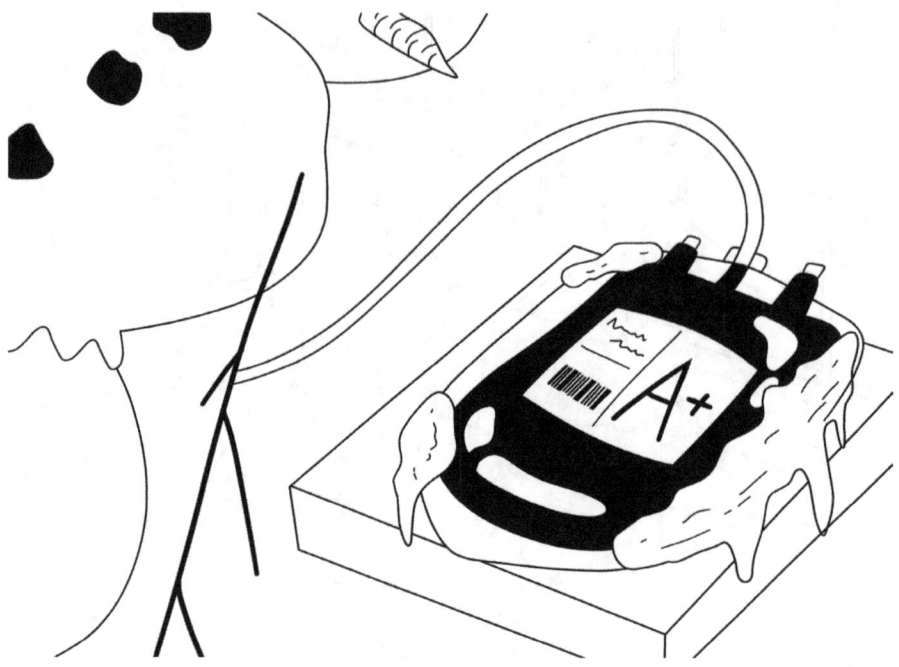

"In cold blood" is an expression that refers to a reprehensible act. For example, when someone is killed for no reason, they are killed "in cold blood." The origin of this phrase can be tied back to 1600s medicine. During that time, it was believed that a person's emotions were connected to the state of their internal fluids. It was a common belief that blood got hotter when someone is angry. Therefore, people with no emotion or regret were thought to have cold blood.

9. When pigs fly

The saying "when pigs fly" is a way of expressing one's disbelief that something is possible. We can also use it as a humorous or even taunting response to someone's prediction when we want to let them know that we consider it impossible. For example, in the sentence, "Yeah, your team will win… when pigs fly!" The speaker is saying that the other person's team will never win. This phrase is categorized as an adynaton, a figure of speech in the form of extreme hyperbole in order to imply complete impossibility. Different versions of this adynaton can be found in various cultures such as "when cows fly" in Finnish or "when hens will have teeth" in French. The expression is derived from a centuries-old Scottish proverb, although its most famous use is in Lewis Carroll's *Alice's Adventures in Wonderland*.

10. Stir up a hornet's nest

To "stir up a hornet's nest" refers to an activity that could result in a negative outcome or provoke someone's negative reaction. We usually apply the phrase "don't stir up a hornet's nest!" when someone is continually behaving in a way that will cause trouble, or to describe someone's actions as risky or instigating. This phrase can be found in *Amphitruo*, a play written by Plautus (200 B.C.), in which the character of Sosia uses it to alert Amphitryon not to get in trouble by arguing with his wife. In English, it can be traced back to the 18th century.

Did you know?

March 1 was designated as the New Year in the early Roman calendar. It had ten months, which is still reflected in some of the names of the months. For example, September through to December, our ninth through to twelfth months, were originally positioned as the seventh through tenth months. *Septum* is Latin for seven, *Octo* is eight, *Novem* is nine, and *Decem* is ten.

Wombats are the only animal whose poop is cube-shaped. This is due to how their intestines form the feces. The animals then stack the cubes to mark their territory.

Eating parts of a pufferfish can kill you because, as a defense mechanism to ward off predators, it contains a deadly chemical called "tetrodotoxin." There's enough in one pufferfish to kill thirty people and there's no antidote. Still, pufferfish, called "fugu," is a highly-prized delicacy in Japan, but can only be prepared by highly-trained chefs.

Early humans used persistence hunting, a technique similarly used by hyenas, wolves and spiders. It involved tracking fast-moving prey over long distances. Humans were partly protected from overheating via exertion because they could sweat, allowing them to endure long runs. That way, they wore down the prey before catching and killing it.

11. Joined at the Hip

To be "joined at the hip" means to be inseparable. We use this idiom as an illustrative and often endearing way of saying that two people are extremely close to each other. One origin idea of this phrase is related to twin brothers Chang and Eng Bunker (1811–1874) who were born with their hips attached. They became recognized for being conjoined twins. The first figurative application of the phrase can be traced back to an article in 1963 from the *Pasadena Star-News* that stated: "The two organizations were so closely knit, they were practically joined at the hip."

12. Knock on Wood

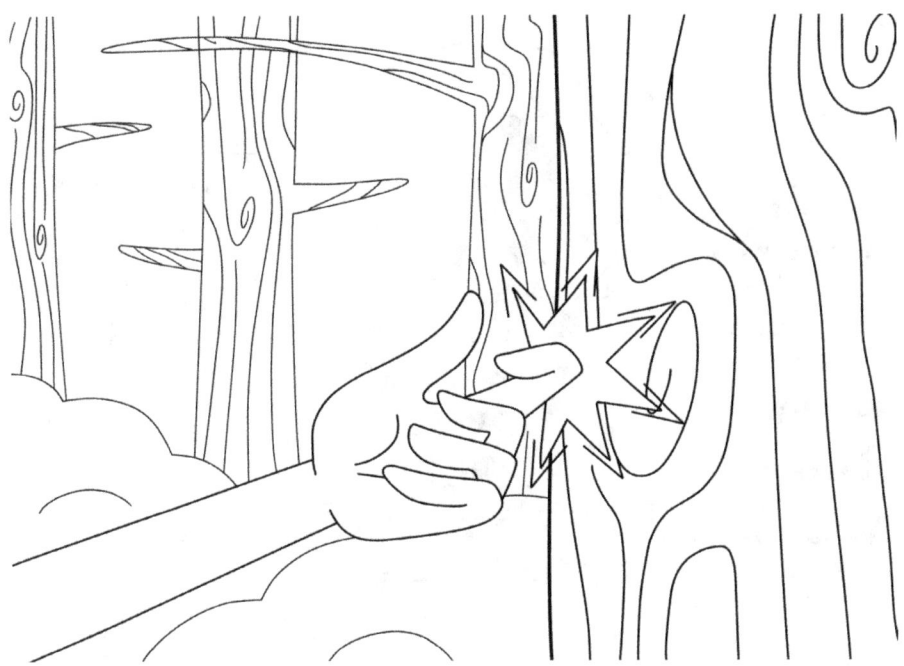

To "knock on wood" is to hope for good luck or good karma. We use this phrase when we want to "invite" good luck to follow us in whatever we're planning to do. People often literally knock on something wooden while saying this expression, as a form of a superstitious ritual that will bring them good fortune. This phrase is thought to come from the ancient Indo-Europeans. People at that time believed the trees housed various spirits, so when you touched the tree, you were given the luck, protection, or blessing of the spirit within the tree.

13. Fat chance

The phrase "fat chance" is a way of sarcastically stating the impossibility of something. When someone tells you that there's a "fat chance" of something happening, they are telling you that there is no chance whatsoever. The origin of this idiom is vague. There are several newspaper articles from the end of the 19th century that used the term "fat chance" which meant "big chance" since the word fat implies that something is ripe and rich. Somewhere along the way, it would seem that the meaning of the expression became the opposite of the word.

14. A SMOOTH SEA NEVER MADE A SKILLED SAILOR

This proverb conveys that life without hardship and the absence of challenges can't help us to develop our character. It's through difficult situations and various temptations that we become more mature and capable. The phrase "smooth sea" represents the easy path through life, while "skilled sailor" represents our virtue and strength of character. This expression is attributed to Franklin D. Roosevelt, the 32nd United States president, but its origin is African.

15. IN THE LOOP

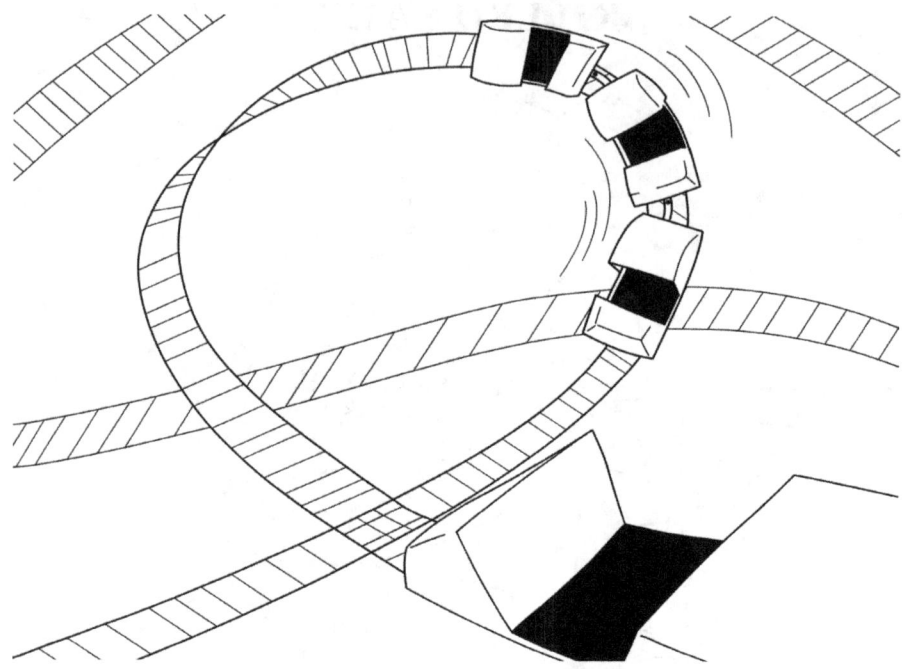

To be "in the loop" means to be aware of particular information. This expression is often formulated as "to stay in the loop," which means to stay informed and acquainted with all the relative aspects within a certain context. In the same way, being "out of the loop" means that a person is not keeping up with the latest information or trends. The origin of this idiom can be traced back to military terminology. In the military, many commanding officers used the phrase "keep everyone in the loop" in the context of passing information to other soldiers to ensure that they were informed.

16. Miss the Boat

When someone has "missed the boat," it means that they have missed their chance to do something by being indecisive or slow to act. However, this idiom can also be used when a person fails to understand something; in this case, we can say that they have "missed the boat" on it. The phrase was first used in a very literal way in Britain when people would miss their boat and be late for their trip. In the 1970s, another popular idiom, "the ship has sailed," was often used interchangeably with this one.

17. Get the Wrong End of the Stick

A person who has "got the wrong end of the stick" has misunderstood something. We use this expression in a situation when a person has the wrong idea about something that's being explained to them. The imagery of this phrase comes from a walking stick which, when held upside down, doesn't help the one holding it. The original 15th-century version of the phrase was "the worse end of the staff" but it changed to the existing idiom in the late 19th century.

18. Ahead of the curve

A person who is "ahead of the curve" has an advantage compared to others. It can refer to being more prepared, more capable than others, or having an innovative thought before others come up with it. We can also use this expression for a person that has managed to predict something that others could not. This phrase can be found in the *Anchorage Daily News* report from May 22, 1974, during President Nixon's administration, stating that the president and his inner circle used the term.

19. Back to Square One

"Back to square one" means returning to the initial starting point. This idiom is commonly used to describe a moment when a process that was advancing in the desired way was stopped, canceled, and brought back to its initial stage, usually by a negative event. The phrase "back to square one" was first used in the 1930s in soccer radio play-by-play. The commentators that were doing the game broadcasts would split the football field into marked grids so that they could explain the plays more easily. The grid that was closest to the home team's goal was marked as "square one." Therefore, if the home team was starting their play from their goal line, the play was called "being back at square one."

20. Bull in a china shop

When a person is like a "bull in a china shop," it means that they are very clumsy. We use this idiom to point out that someone is uncoordinated but in a humorous and kind way. The idea for this phrase comes from the imagery of the bull, a giant animal, in a china shop full of fragile materials made of porcelain. On the other hand, this phrase can also be used to represent someone who is big and brutish. In this case, it doesn't describe a person in a kind way, but rather someone who is too rough. Some sources state that it stems from Frederick Marryat's novel called *Jacob Faithful* published in the year 1834.

Did You Know?

Cartoonist Mort Walker, the creator of Beetle Bailey, came up with images for the things we often see in comics and cartoons. "Briffit" is the dust cloud a character makes when he runs away quickly; "plewds" are the beads of sweat when a character is under duress; and "grawlix" are symbols such as "#@*%" that stand in for curse words.

A mash-up of two words making a new word (such as breakfast and lunch into brunch, or motel from motor and hotel) is called a "portmanteau." In case you're wondering, the word "portmanteau" itself is a portmanteau; it's a compound word that refers to a dual-sided suitcase.

What's inside a Kit Kat? Broken Kit Kats that are damaged during production—they get ground up and go between the wafers, along with cocoa and sugar.

Archaeologists found a ring inside a Viking grave in the 1800s in Sweden that had "For Allah" engraved on it, showing there was linked trade between the Islamic world and the Swedish Vikings from over a thousand years ago.

21. Mind your own beeswax

"Mind your own beeswax" basically means to "mind your own business." In the literal phrase "mind your own business," "business" was converted to "beeswax" to make it less rude and unpleasant. The word "beeswax" has a similar sound as "business" and stands as a proxy for the original word, and even though the message is the same, the form is more socially acceptable. However, there are additional theories about the origin of this expression. The most interesting one tells that beeswax was used as makeup for people who had scars from smallpox during the 18th and 19th centuries and "mind your own beeswax" was a response if someone would rudely stare at their scarred faces.

22. NO SPRING CHICKEN

When we say that someone is "no spring chicken," we are saying that that person is no longer young. We usually use this idiom in situations when someone's appearance and behavior create an impression that they are much younger than they really are. In the 17th century, chickens that were born in the spring brought in more money than other chickens because they were younger than those that had lived through the winter. As a result, many farmers tried to sell their old chickens as "spring chickens" which led to people creating the phrase, "that is no spring chicken!"

23. ACROSS THE BOARD

If something is "across the board," that means that it includes or affects everything or everyone within a certain group. For example, having an "across the board" pay raise means that everyone in a certain company will have their paychecks increased. This idiom is commonly used to describe processes that affect all of the people within a party. The expression's origin comes from horse racing as it described a form of betting. An "across the board" bet meant that equal stakes of money were bet on the same horse to either win, place, or show (betting on all categories that were on the board). The idiom was first used in print with this purpose in the *Atlanta Constitution* in November 1901.

24. Stand your ground

To "stand one's ground" means to not retreat, falter, or surrender. We can use this idiom in several different contexts. Firstly, "stand your ground" is a common military and war-related phrase, referring to soldiers remaining in their position when the enemy attacking may be stronger or have overwhelming force. In everyday situations, it means someone is ready to defend their intentions, behaviors, or opinions, even when there is opposition by other people. In the world of law, the phrase represents a principle that allows a person to use deadly force in self-defense without first trying to retreat. The first "Stand Your Ground" law in America came to pass in Florida in 2005 and they now exists in over thirty states.

25. Everything but the Kitchen Sink

This is a phrase that is jokingly used when someone has overpacked for a trip. In this situation, we can say that they have packed "everything but the kitchen sink." It translates as "everything imaginable" or "much more than necessary." The first use of this idiom can be traced back to the early 20th century in the newspaper *The Syracuse Herald*. The phrase "everything was thrown at the enemy, but the kitchen sink," was popularly used during World War II in descriptions of battles. However, there's an even older expression, "everything but the kitchen stove," which dates from the 19th century and could be this one's predecessor.

26. Drop like flies

The expression "drop like flies" means that people or animals are falling dead or ill very quickly in large numbers. While the origin of this idiom isn't entirely certain, it is clear that this phrase represents the short lifespan of a fly. Namely, flies have a maximum lifespan of twenty-eight days, so they die and drop very quickly and easily. One of the recorded uses of this phrase was the 1902 *Atlanta Constitution* newspaper reports on a fire that broke out that, "I saw men and women rushing back and forth within the flames. They would run along, then came the choking smoke and they would drop like dead flies."

27. Every cloud has a silver lining

This proverb states that we can find something hopeful and comforting in every challenging or sad situation, even if we can't see it at the moment. We usually use this proverbial saying for the purpose of comforting someone who is going through hardship or to inspire them to "look at the bright side." This idiom has most likely been traced back to 1634 when John Milton stated, "Was I deceived or did a sable cloud turn forth her silver lining on the night?"

28. A STITCH IN TIME SAVES NINE

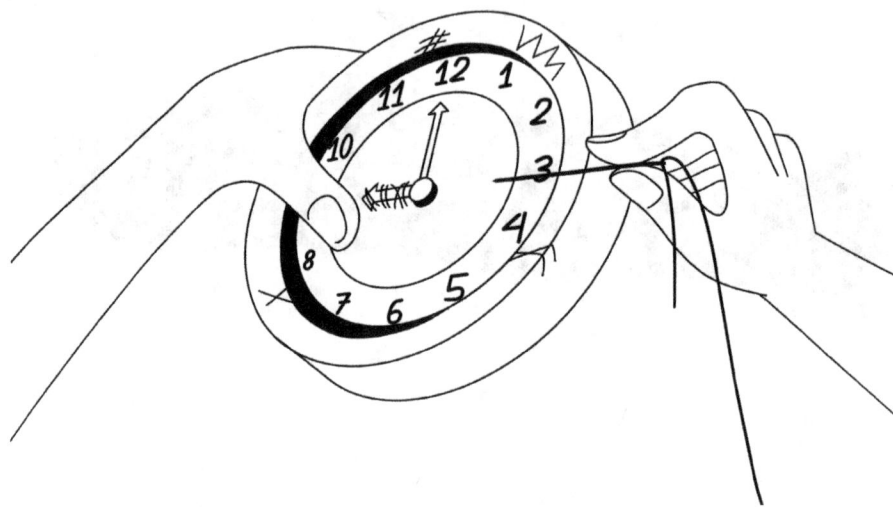

This proverb states that it is better to resolve a problematic situation when it is still a little nuisance than to wait until it becomes a serious crisis. We usually use this proverbial expression when we want to urge someone to take care of a problem immediately before it grows or to simply point out that such an approach to life can save us a lot of time and trouble in the future. This phrase was first seen in *Thomas Fuller's Gnomologia: A Collection of the Proverbs, Maxims, and Adages That Inspired Benjamin Franklin and Poor Richard's Almanack* in 1732.

29. Kick the can down the road

To "kick the can down the road" means to put off facing a difficult situation or making an important decision. We use this idiom to describe a situation when a person is procrastinating on something vital. Often, it's used when a person has been delaying for a considerable time or when dawdling is typical for that person. The expression originates from a game that was played during the Great Depression. This game was a version of 'hide n seek,' with the rule that kicking the can will release all the players that have been captured during that round. It isn't clear how that translated to its modern meaning. It's more plausible to connect the meaning to the imagery of kicking trash on the street out of sight so it becomes someone else's concern.

30. CALL THE SHOTS

A person who is "calling the shots" is a person in a position of leadership who makes important decisions that will affect a certain situation. We use this idiom to describe an action of making important decisions or to single out a person who is in charge. This expression was part of the military vocabulary. Namely, during marksmanship training, it was common practice to declare where a fired shot had hit the target. Also, some shooters called where they were intending to shoot beforehand. The phrase with its modern meaning was first used in print in the 1960s.

Did you know?

There was a medieval belief that crocodiles shed tears of sadness while they killed and consumed their prey. From this myth, which dates back as far as the 14th century, the term "crocodile tears" is actually derived. The belief started from a book called "The Travels of Sir John Mandeville" and, later on, it was found in the works of Shakespeare.

The teddy bear is named after President Theodore Roosevelt. After he refused to shoot a captured black bear on a hunt, a stuffed-animal maker decided to create a bear and name it after the president.

Play-Doh started out as a wallpaper cleaner before the head of the struggling company realized the non-toxic material made a good modeling clay for children and rebranded it.

The sister ship of the Titanic, the Olympic, offered to take in the survivors when the Titanic sank. The Captain of the Titanic rejected the offer as he was afraid that this would cause panic among the survivors seeing a virtual mirror image of the ship that had just sank, asking them to come on board.

31. ON THE CARDS

If something is "on the cards," it means that it is meant to happen or most likely going to happen. In America, the same idiom is referred to as "in the cards" while in Britain, the phrase is referred to as "on the cards." The origin of this idiom can be drawn back to the 1800s when tarot cards and fortune-telling were rising in popularity. When something was written on the cards in tarot or fortune, it was meant to tell your future. It can also be seen in a poem written by Charles Churchill titled *Independence*.

32. Knock your socks off

If something "knocked your socks off," it means that you were impressed by it. We use this idiom to describe something exciting or when we want to share our enthusiasm with others, to let them know that they are about to see something amazing. This idiom was originally used in the southern regions of America in the 1940s. During that time, the phrase meant to beat someone in a fight, but it changed from winning a fight to impressing someone.

33. A BED OF ROSES

A person laying in a "bed of roses" is in a very comfortable or luxurious position. We use this idiom to describe someone's favorable circumstances. One of the earliest written forms of this expression can be found in a poem titled *The Passionate Shepherd to His Love* which was published in 1599. The poem stated:

> And I will make thee beds of roses
> And a thousand fragrant posies,
> A cap of flowers, and a kirtle
> Embroidered all with leaves of myrtle.

34. IN A NUTSHELL

The phrase "in a nutshell" refers to telling a story concisely or quickly. We use this idiom when we want to let someone know that what we are about to tell them is a shortened and simplified version of the entire account. This idiom's first use can be found in a book titled *Natural History* by the Roman writer Pliny the Elder. In the book, Pliny describes Homer's *Iliad* as being copied in so tiny a hand that it could fit "in a nutshell." However, it was later found that Shakespeare had used this phrase in Hamlet with the meaning of "something compact," while William Thackeray (British novelist) used it in its present meaning in *The Second Funeral of Napoleon* in 1841.

35. Walking on Eggshells

When a person is "walking on eggshells," it means that they have to be careful with what they are doing or saying. We use this idiom to describe a situation when a touchy subject is being discussed and people have to watch what they are saying and how they are behaving so as to not offend anyone. This phrase came into use in the 1800s after its predecessor "walking on eggs." The phrase stems from the imagery of walking on something as fragile as eggs, which emphasizes how careful that person has to be.

36. Spanner in the works

To throw a "spanner in the works" is to, purposefully or not, sabotage something, cause its delay or interruption, or to interfere with a certain process or procedure. The phrase can be found in several forms - "put/throw a spanner/wrench in the works/wheels/gears." Its first recorded print is found in *The Parliamentary Debates* of the New Zealand Parliament, 1932: "Of course, every honorable member has a right to express his opinions, even of a critical nature, but I do think we should expect them to help and not throw a spanner in the gears."

37. Brownie points

When a person is trying to make a good impression on someone or establish a positive relationship, they try to earn their respect and trust by doing something nice for them. The term "brownie points" is a representation of all of our nice gestures for someone, which make them think positively of us. This idiom originated from the points earned for different accomplishments by the Brownies, which were the youngest girls within the Girl Scouts. In the mid-20th century, it became an expression used for achievements within any relationship with a person or a group.

38. Fair and square

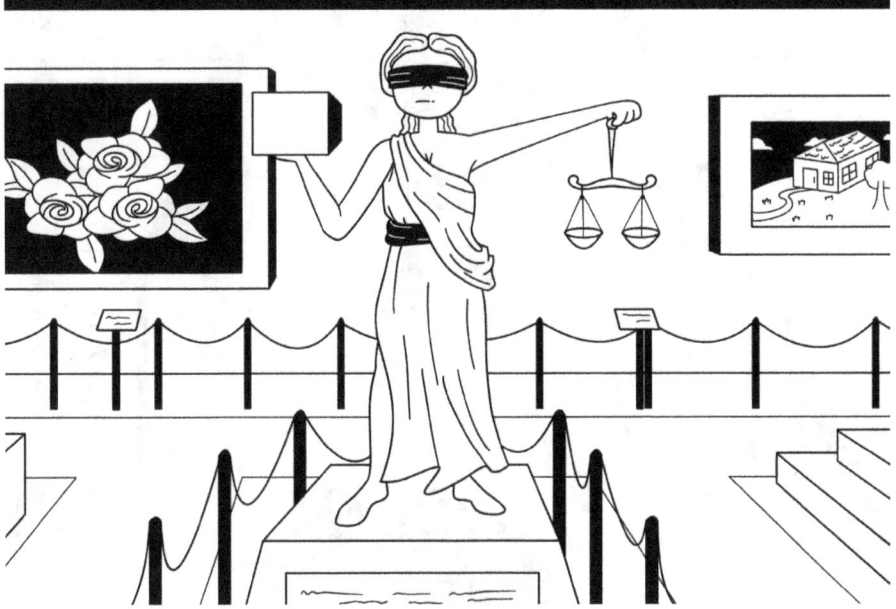

"Fair and square" means that something is done according to the rules or the agreement between two parties. We use this expression to describe a situation in which every agreed-upon rule has been honored and to state that the outcome is acceptable because it is fair. This rhyming phrase can be traced back to the 1600s and it was used in reference to sports or contests (it is still often used in the same context). The initial phrase was "fair and honest," but over time, the word "square" slowly replaced "honest."

39. Laughing stock

The "laughing stock" of a certain group is the person who is being laughed at by everyone else in the group. We use this expression to state that a person is being ridiculed, made fun of, and even humiliated by others. Calling someone the "laughing stock" of the group can be insulting. The origin of this expression could be related to the stocks: a punishment method that included the guilty person having their head and hands trapped inside a wooden stock. Other people would then ridicule them and throw objects at them for their crimes.

40. Keep your nose clean

The phrase "keep one's nose clean" refers to that person's tendency to stay out of trouble and maintain their good reputation. We use this expression to state that our priority is to have a clean reputation and keep our conscience clean. This phrase was originally worded as "keeping your hands clean." When it was used in England in the 18th century, it related to avoiding corruption. When it was adopted in the United States as "keep your nose clean," it meant to keep your nose out of other people's business.

Did you know?

Michelin stars are highly coveted by elite and upscale restaurants all around the world. They are actually given out by the Michelin tire company, the same one whose mascot is the marshmallow-like Michelin Man.

The longest place name in the world, at eighty five letters, is "Taumatawhakatangihangakoauauotamateaturipukakapikimaungahoronukupokaiwhenuakitanatahu," in New Zealand. Locals just call it Taumata Hill.

The world record for the holder of the most world records is Ashrita Furman, who's set more than six hundred records and currently holds more than 200. His records have ranged from fastest mile on a pogo stick, longest time to hula hoop underwater, and greatest distance traveled on a bicycle balancing a milk bottle on the head.

The first housewarming parties were literally held to warm houses and send the spirits away. All guests would bring over pieces of wood and they would light fires in every fireplace in the new home. There was a belief that empty houses would attract spirits and ghosts, so when people would move in, they would warm the house to send the spirits away.

41. Elephant in the Room

When there is an "elephant in the room," it means that there is an obvious issue that no one wants or dares to address. We use this widely known idiom in situations when everyone in a certain group is avoiding a subject, usually because it is touchy and delicate, which causes everyone to feel awkward and unpleasant. Addressing the "elephant in the room," which is also how the phrase is commonly applied, is stating that the subject has to be discussed because it is apparent to everyone and there is no point in pretending. The origin of it stems from the imagery of a huge animal such as an elephant in a narrow space, which would make it impossible to be unnoticed.

42. Green thumb

To have a "green thumb" means that you are good with plants and wildlife. This is an expression that describes people who have an affinity towards gardening, growing plants, and who enjoy spending their time in green environments. This phrase comes from the fact that people who regularly handle plants get their thumbs stained green from algae growing on the exterior of pottery. Because of this, if someone has a "green thumb," others would know that they are often involved with plants.

43. Jump on the Bandwagon

When someone starts liking a celebrity who is at the peak of their fame or starts cheering on a team that is currently winning, they are "jumping on the bandwagon." This expression describes some people's tendency to like, support, and cheer individuals or groups that are currently the most popular, just because the majority of people feel the same. This phrase was first heard in the 1848 presidential campaign of Zachary Taylor. Dan Rice was a popular circus clown at the time who invited Taylor to his circus bandwagon. As he grew in popularity, people began to tell his opponents that they should "jump on the bandwagon" as well.

44. An ace up one's sleeve

If someone has an "ace up their sleeve," that means that they hold a secret advantage in reserve that they can use at any time and without others anticipating it. An ace up one's sleeve can be an object, a skill, or a piece of information that they secretly have, that could better their position in various contexts. The term "to have an ace up one's sleeve" originates from mid-1800s gambling games. Specifically, in a game of poker, the ace card is the most powerful card you can be dealt. Therefore, someone holding an ace up their sleeve would have a secret advantage that they could use to win the game.

45. Out on the Town

Going "out on the town" means that a person is going out to bars and clubs, probably visiting several places for a night out. Usually, people say they are going "out on the town" when they are going out to a party or to have fun. This phrase is thought to have originated in the 1700s, but it didn't gain popularity until the 1900s when a stage show titled "On The Town" was performed in 1944 and a film by the same name, starring Gene Kelly, Frank Sinatra, and Ann Miller, came out in 1949. Since then, it became a common way of expressing our plans of going out and our enthusiasm about it.

46. Wouldn't be caught dead

If a person says that they "wouldn't be caught dead" doing something, it means that they find that action reprehensible or shameful. For example, people often say that they "wouldn't be caught dead" wearing a piece of clothing because they dislike it so much that they would feel embarrassed if they were wearing it. The phrase is meant to convey such an extreme embarrassment of something, that we wouldn't want to be associated with it, even if we were dead. This phrase first appeared near the beginning of the 20th century.

47. Born with a Silver Spoon in Your Mouth

If a person was "born with a silver spoon in their mouth," it means that they were born into a wealthy household and have grown up leading a privileged and comfortable life. We usually use this idiom to point out someone's high social and material status, but with certain disapproval, because their wealth and comfort have made them spoiled or lazy. The phrase contains a reference to a spoon because old spoons were made of wood, so only those who were wealthy owned silver spoons. The expression first occurred in print in English in 1719, in Peter Anthony Motteux's translation of the novel *Don Quixote*.

48. Fan the flames

To "fan the flames" means to amplify already strong feelings or to intensify an already tense situation. These feelings can be positive (like love/infatuation), or negative (like anger/resentment). In both cases, if a person does something to stir up those feelings, we can say that they have "fanned the flames." The first use of this idiom in writing was by Charles Dickens in *The Old Curiosity Shop* when he said, "Fan the sinking flames of hilarity with the wing of friendship."

49. Down to the Wire

"Down to the wire" is an expression used to describe a suspenseful situation that's not going to be resolved or decided until the last moment. This idiom is most commonly applied in sports and competitions, where games are often close and the result can be decided at the last second. This phrase is believed to have come from horse racing where there was a wire hung across the finish line. The winner was decided by the horse that touched the wire first, so when the race was close, the result was going to be "down to the wire."

50. Bare bones

When something is "bare bones," it means that it includes only its basic or bare elements. We use this idiom to describe something that includes only what's necessary; for example, the "bare bones" of a novel's plot represent only the key points of its story. This expression stems from the 1700s and, originally, it was related to the description of someone extremely skinny which made it possible to notice the outline of their bones through their skin. Over time, that meaning transformed to breaking something down to its more essential elements.

DID YOU KNOW?

Competitive art used to be an Olympic sport. Between 1912 and 1948, the international sporting events awarded medals for music, painting, sculpture, and architecture.

English as a second language is four times more common than as a native one. While more people speak English as a second language, nearly three times more people speak Mandarin Chinese natively. Nearly two billion people are learning English as a second language while only 350 million people natively speak it.

When Genghis Khan died, his successors killed anyone who witnessed his funeral procession in order to keep his burial place a secret. About 800 soldiers were massacred as well as 2,000 other people. The location of his tomb is unknown to this day.

The lyrebird can mimic almost any sound it hears. Wildlife watchers have recorded the Australian species copying not only other birds but artificial sounds such as car alarms, camera shutters, and even chainsaws.

51. In the Nick of Time

"In the nick of time" means just in time. We use this idiom when something has happened in the last possible moment before it was too late, usually when someone arrives or when something is done just before the deadline. This expression originates from the 16th century. However, its predecessor was the phrase "pudding time" because pudding was the dish served first in medieval Britain. To arrive at "pudding time" meant to get there at the start of the feast, just in time to dine.

52. At Odds

When two parties are "at odds" about something, that means that they are in conflict or disagreement. We use this idiom to point out that two people or two groups have different stances on an issue or when someone is not approving of a certain action, process, or objective. It's appropriate to say that people are at odds either about/over something, or at odds with each other (if the disagreement lies between people). The origin of this idiom is believed to come from the concept of odd or even. When things were even, they were the same. When things were odd, they were the opposite.

53. Hissy fit

When someone throws a "hissy fit," they are throwing a tantrum as a child would. The expression can be synonymous with an angry outburst. This idiom originated in the 1900s, though it first began as just "hissy." It is believed that the word came as a shorter version of the word "hysterical." Other origin theories make a connection between the phrase and hissing noises related to being angry or aggressive.

54. The devil is beating his wife

"The devil is beating his wife" is an idiom that describes a weather occurrence commonly known as a sun shower, when it's raining and the sun is shining at the same time. This expression can be linked to folkloric tales of various cultures. Most of these tales include animals or tricksters being related or getting married to the devil. For example, when a sun shower happens, Hungarians say "the devil is beating his wife with a walking stick," while the French expression is "the devil is beating his wife and marrying his daughter." The imagery of the phrase can be related to the symbols of the devil spitting fire, represented by the sun shining, and his crying wife represented by the rain.

55. Add fuel to the fire

To "add fuel to the fire" means to further instigate an already tense situation that's usually filled with negative emotion, like anger and frustration. We use this phrase when someone's actions don't de-escalate a crisis but make it even more complicated instead. We call those actions "adding fuel to the fire." This expression is of Latin origin and can be traced back to around the year 1 A.D. The Roman historian Livy used this expression in his *History of Rome*.

56. Buckle down

To "buckle down" means to focus and take your work or situation seriously. For example, if a person has a short deadline on an important project at work, they will "buckle down," concentrate, and promptly get their work done. While this modern phrase comes from the United States, there was an older phrase that was similar in Britain that was said as "buckle to." This phrase dates back to the 18th century in a story by John Arbuthnot where it read, "Squire South buckles to, to assist his friend Nic." In America, the first time the modern phrase was in the *Atlantic Monthly* with a quote: "If he would only buckle down to serious study."

57. Red tape

Running into "red tape" means that a person is being stopped or slowed in doing something, by rules or regulations. It is most commonly used to refer to unnecessary paperwork in certain processes, particularly in legal or bureaucratic work. It is commonly believed that the phrase came from King Charles V, King of Spain and Holy Roman Emperor, in the early 16th century. During his time, red tape was used to single out the most important documents that required immediate attention by the Council of State and separate them from the other less important issues. That way, the red tape became a symbol of speeding up administrative processes.

58. On Top of the World

Being "on top of the world" means that a person feels good, confident, and happy with themselves and how their life is going. We use this phrase to describe a feeling of pleasure with oneself, usually because the person has achieved something that they have dreamed of. This phrase has been around since the 1920s as many writers would use it in their work. It was most commonly phrased as "sitting on top of the world," but it was eventually shortened to just "on top of the world."

59. Pay the piper

To "pay the piper" means to pay the consequences for one's actions, usually self-indulgent or irresponsible behavior. We use this idiom to describe a situation when someone is feeling the negative effects of their mistakes or to warn someone that their current behavior can lead to bad outcomes and that they will have to "pay the piper" sooner or later. This expression can be traced back to the 1680s from the story *The Pied Piper of Hamelin*. In the story, a man with a pipe appears in town and states that he can solve the townspeople's problem for a price. Once they paid, he led all of the rats out of town.

60. Play cat and mouse

When two parties "play cat and mouse," it means that one or both parties are saying or doing confusing and contradictory things, changing their opinions and behavior towards the other side, or acting deceitfully. The phrase is commonly applied to people and how they treat each other. Namely, when people often change their attitude towards each other, frequently arguing and making up - we say that they are playing cat and mouse. This idiom can also be applied to other kinds of contradictory, avoidant, or deceitful behaviors. The phrase originates from the imagery of a cat's hunt for the mouse. Cats will often play with their prey until it's tired or torment it until it dies. It has been applied in writing since 1675 and can be found in the Brothers Grimm *Fairy Tales*.

Did You Know?

The Great Fire of London left more than 70,000 people homeless after destroying more than 13,300 buildings in 1666. Despite all the destruction, only six deaths were verified in official records.

As far back as 200 B.C., the Han Dynasty of China drilled for natural gas, transported it in pipelines and gas containers, and burned it on stoves, though natural gas wasn't in common use worldwide until the 1800s.

Moonflowers actually bloom in response to the moon. Sunflowers will follow the sun as it moves across the sky, but their lunar counterparts only open after nightfall or on cloudy days.

The first Roman fire brigade consisted of 500 men and it was created by Marcus Licinius Crassus. The brigade would show up at a burning building and start haggling with the property owner over the price of their services. If Crassus didn't get a high enough payment offer, he would literally let the building burn to the ground, then he would ask the owner to let him buy it for a fraction of its original value.

61. Let the chips fall where they may

To "let the chips fall where they may" means to let something happen regardless of the consequences. This phrase originated in America in the 1800s. It was first used in reference to chopping wood. Namely, woodcutters used the expression to let each other know that they should proceed with their work without worrying where the chips of wood would end up.

62. Mumbo jumbo

"That's a load of mumbo jumbo!" - this phrase means that something is meaningless or incomprehensible to the observer. It was most commonly associated with religious customs and rituals that people of different religions didn't understand. Sadly, this phrase came to be out of human ignorance. The idiom originates from the Mandingo word "Maamajomboo," which refers to a masked male dancer who was part of African religious rituals. However, people of other religions looked at this character and didn't understand his meaning, thus changing the original name Maamajomboo to the modern "mumbo jumbo."

63. Loose cannon

When someone is a "loose cannon," it means that they are unpredictable and that others don't know what they're going to do next. The expression usually has a negative connotation attached to it because people with such an impulsive character may cause harm to those around them due to their unpredictability. The phrase stems from naval terminology. Back in the 17th century, warships would carry cannons as their primary weapon. These cannons had to be secured with rollers and ropes, and those that became loose and rolled around the deck would present a danger for the crew of the ship if they fired and hurt someone or damaged the vessel.

64. A SLAP ON THE WRIST

Getting "a slap on the wrist" means getting a mild punishment, usually for a larger action or crime, that probably deserved a more severe penalty. The origin of this expression is most likely 18th century England, where the term "slap" was used both literally and figuratively. In 18th century England, punishments for crimes would often be quite severe and of a physical nature. Therefore, a slap on the wrist would have been seen as a light punishment.

65. Low hanging fruit

"Low hanging fruit" is a term that is most commonly used in workplaces or in business for tasks and procedures that can be easily accomplished. We use this idiom to describe work that takes little to no effort. The phrase comes from farmwork and harvesting because the fruit that didn't require harvesters to climb on ladders was the easiest to be picked up. That idea was then translated into any effortless work.

66. HEAD OVER HEELS

To fall "head over heels" in literal meaning refers to turning over completely while going forward, like doing a somersault. However, the more common practise is its metaphorical use, which refers to falling completely in love with someone. To be "head over heels" for a person means to be deeply in love with them. This phrase can be traced back to the 1300s and its predecessor "heels over head" which meant hanging upside down. The phrase was transformed to "head over heels" in the 1700s and started to relate to its present meaning in the 1800s.

67. THE ELEVENTH HOUR

Doing something at "the eleventh hour" means doing it at the last minute. We use this phrase whenever something has been done just before the deadline, like the sentence, "I got there at the eleventh hour," meaning that the speaker was almost late, but made the appointment. The phrase "eleventh hour" has a Biblical background. It comes from a chapter in the *Gospel of Matthew* in which some last-minute workers, who were employed long after the rest, are paid the same salary. Even though they were employed after eleven hours of work, they weren't too late to receive their pay.

68. Hot Potato

"Hot potato" refers to a controversial issue or situation which is awkward to deal with. We use this idiom for a topic that is touchy to discuss or a situation that doesn't have an easy resolution. This expression originates from the imagery of holding or handling a hot potato. One would have to get rid of the potato quickly so they wouldn't get burned, or avoid such a situation completely. Handling a difficult situation or a controversial subject can feel like juggling a hot potato. This term can be traced back to the mid-1800s.

69. Old habits die hard

This proverb states that habits that a person has are not easy to get rid of. It can also mean that someone's behavior is not easily changeable. The most common examples for this expression are found in situations when people are trying to quit smoking, change their diet, or modify some other deeply rooted behavior. We usually use it when these negative behavioral patterns have been present for such a long time, that breaking them represents a great challenge. In some cases, the speaker is trying to express their disbelief that the person in question is capable of change. This proverbial phrase can be traced back to an article written by Benjamin Franklin in 1758.

70. IN MINT CONDITION

Something that is "in mint condition" is completely preserved in its original state. This expression is most applicable to collectors of objects who are very particular about the condition of their collectibles. A collectible object in mint condition has a higher value in the world of collecting. The origin of the phrase stems from the meaning of the word "mint." To "mint" something is to form a shape from a piece of metal. Therefore, to be "in mint condition" is to look fresh and crisp as a newly minted coin. This phrase can be traced back to an 1895 Scottish newspaper that stated that a postage stamp that was in mint condition was being sold for a higher price.

Did you know?

In the Satere-Mawe Indian culture, there is an initiation ritual for thirteen-year-old boys that consists of making them wear gloves made of bullet ants for ten minutes. Although they are repeatedly bitten, which is incredibly painful, they must not cry out if they want to be declared a man.

The Great Sphinx of Giza was constructed out of a single chunk of soft limestone bedrock. This magnificent monument stands over sixty five feet (twenty meters) high, almost two hundred and forty feet (seventy-four meters) long, and over sixty-two feet (nineteen meters) wide.

A team of six women programmed the first digital computer. While historians have only recently recognized their achievements (or many female discoveries credited to men), the female mathematicians participated in a World War II program, coding instructions into the revolutionary Electronic Numerical Integrator and Computer (ENIAC).

Cobwebs actually have antifungal and antiseptic properties that keep bacteria away and minimize the chance of infection. In fact, the Greeks and Romans would use cobwebs to treat cuts in ancient times. Soldiers also used them to heal wounds, combining honey and vinegar to clean the lesions, and then covering them with balled-up spider webs.

71. Green with envy

To be "green with envy" means to be very jealous of someone. The expression is used to emphasize the potency of the person's envy and negative emotion. In ancient Greece, the color green was related to sickness, fear, and jealousy. Because of this, the color green became a common symbol of a person being envious. The phrase was further popularized by William Shakespeare in his famous play *Othello* when he wrote, "Beware, my lord, of jealousy; it is the green-eyed monster which doth mock the meat it feeds on."

72. CUT THE CORD

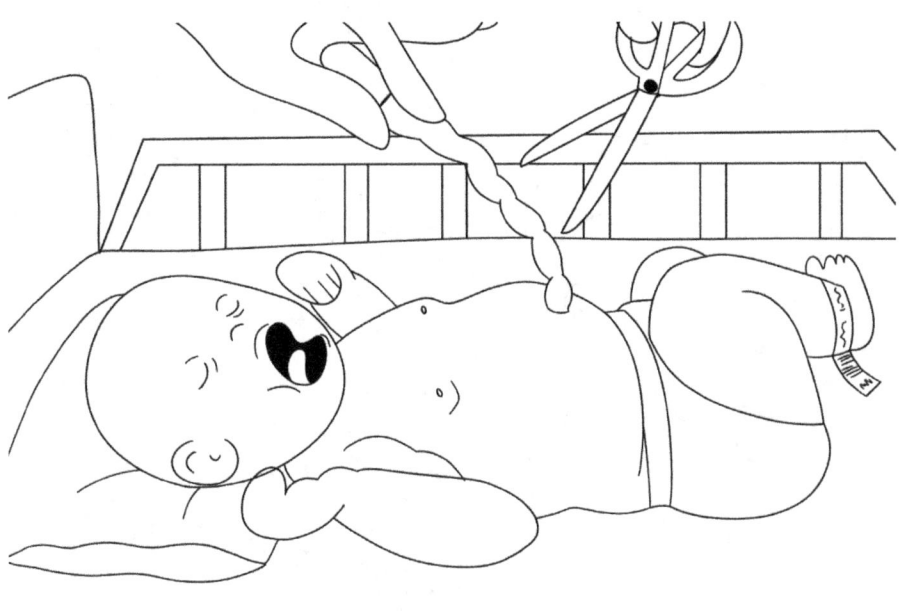

The phrase "cut the cord" means to end a connection with someone or something that had a protective/supportive role in one's life and to stop relying on it. The origin of this phrase stems from the act of human birth. When a baby is born, the umbilical cord that attaches the mother to the baby is cut. Once the cord is cut, the mother's body is no longer providing food through it to the baby. Instead, the baby is living and breathing on its own. Therefore, cutting the cord is a symbol of removing a protective and supportive bond.

73. Keen as mustard

To be "keen as mustard" means to be very excited and interested in something. We use this phrase to highlight someone's enthusiasm. It was first documented in William Walker's work called *Phraseologia Anglo-Latina, or phrases of the English and Latin tongue; together with Paroemiologia Anglo-Latina* in 1672. However, the connection can also be made with the meaning that the word "mustard" had in the early 20th century. The famous sauce was an essential element of roasted beef and became associated with intensity and enthusiasm because of its characteristic strong flavor. Therefore, when something was amazing, the common phrase was: "It's mustard!"

74. Dead as a doornail

To be "as dead as a doornail" is to be utterly dead or devoid of life. This expression can also be applied to an object that has become unusable. For example, a computer that cannot be started anymore because it is broken beyond repair can be called "as dead as a doornail." Furthermore, ideas or plans that are no longer possible can also be described as "dead as a doornail." This phrase was used in the 16th century by William Shakespeare and in Charles Dickens' *A Christmas Carol* in 1843. The expression probably originates from the method of securing doornails hammered into a door by clenching them.

75. Tall story

When we call someone's retelling of something a "tall story," it means that we consider it exaggerated and unnecessarily boastful. We usually use this idiom when we hear a story that's hardly possible or one that we don't believe at all. In that case, we can call it a "tall story," conveying to the person telling it that they should be more truthful in their storytelling.

76. Hit or miss

When something is "hit or miss," it means that it is sometimes successful/good and sometimes not, but we cannot rely on any outcome for certain, nor do we have any control over it. The expression most likely stems from some sort of shooting or throwing. It has been used in its present form since the 16th century, as it can be found in Shakespeare's *Troilus and Cressida*, which quotes: "But hit or miss, our project's life this shape of sense assumes."

77. Rain or shine

If a person is going to do something "rain or shine," it means that they are doing it whether it rains or not. However, the expression can also mean "no matter the obstacles" in some cases. In this instance, the phrase is used to state that the person is persistent about doing something, no matter what happens. The first recorded use of the expression was in 1699 by the writer John Goad.

78. Fight tooth and nail

To "fight tooth and nail" means to fight with all of one's effort and intensity. The phrase can be used to describe a physical fight or a verbal fight, but in both cases, it means that the opposing sides are giving it their all and that the conflict is very intense. This phrase comes from the idea of animals fighting as they use their teeth and nails to take down prey. The expression can be traced back to the 15th century, but connections can also be found between this idiom and the old Latin phrase "toto corpore atque omnibus ungulis" which translates to "all the body and with every nail."

79. Piece of Cake

When something is a "piece of cake," it means that it is easy or requires little effort. A cake being related to something "easy" can be traced back to the 1870s. At that time, competitions called "cakewalks" were a common form of entertainment in the United States. In these contests, people tried to display who could walk the most gracefully. At the end of the competition, the most "graceful" pair would be given a cake as a reward. The tradition died out, and the term "cakewalk" eventually changed into the modern "piece of cake."

80. Where the rubber meets the road

"Where the rubber meets the road" is a phrase that refers to a moment when a theory or idea is put to the test to see if it actually works. It can be translated to "a moment of truth" when things become clear and the observers can finally ascertain which ideas and assumptions were true and which weren't. It can also represent any moment when things become serious. The phrase is probably related to the imagery of the rubber wheels making contact with the road, representing the moment of truth when we can see if a vehicle is reliable or not.

Did You Know?

There's a 107-acre forest made up of a single tree. The "Trembling Giant" in Utah's Fishlake National Forest includes over 47,000 quaking aspen trees that share the same root system. Some scientists estimate it's close to a million years old.

From the 16th century up until the 1960s, Egyptian mummies were actually ground up and used to produce a brown paint color called Mummy Brown. The powder was mixed with white pitch and myrrh to make a rich brown pigment.

The deepest mail box in the world is in a small Japanese fishing town called Susami, according to the Guinness Book of World Records. It's an old-school red mailbox that's located thirty-two feet (ten meters) under water, and divers often place waterproof letters there and they are then collected in regular intervals. The mailbox is quite active, as it receives one to five thousand pieces of mail annually.

It took almost twenty-two years to build the Taj Mahal in India. Construction began in 1632 and finished in 1653. It was built by Emperor Shah Jahan, who was in deep grief over his passing wife, as a tribute to their love.

81. Square peg in a round hole

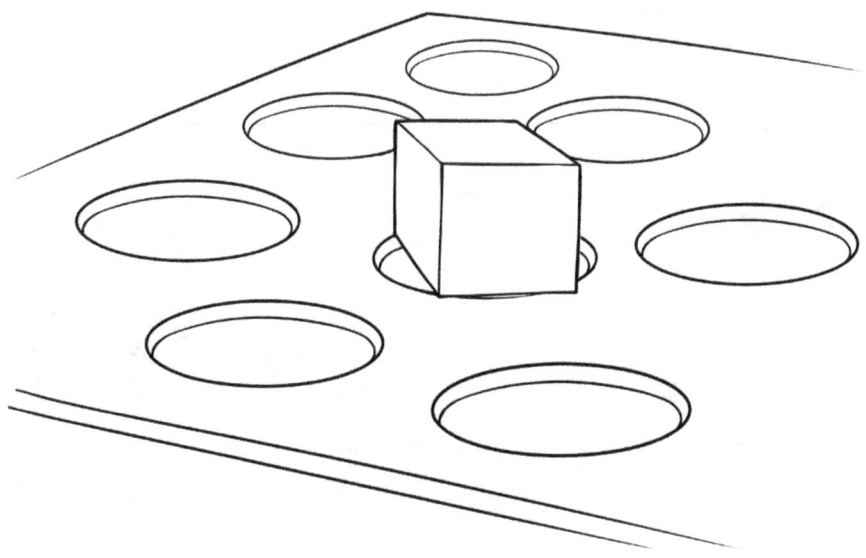

The phrase "square peg in a round hole" refers to a person in a situation unsuited to their abilities or character. Usually, we say that a person feels like a "square peg in a round hole" because they feel inadequate or like a misfit in a certain environment. This expression can be drawn back to the 19th century in England. A British philosopher and cleric by the name of Sydney Smith used it to describe someone who stood out or did not fit into society.

82. Pep talk

A "pep talk" refers to a talk that is meant to motivate or inspire. Usually, before doing something important, people give each other pep talks to encourage each other and better prepare for a coming challenge. Pep talks are common in sports, before games, but also in other competitive environments that require participants to stay motivated and focused. This term probably comes from the word "pepper" which was shortened to "pep" over time. In the 19th century, "pepper" was a symbol of personal energy or spirit. Since it was related to energy and motivation, in time it transformed into the modern phrase "pep talk."

83. Pie in the Sky

A "pie in the sky" refers to pleasant dreams of people that are not likely to come true. We use this idiom to describe a person's hopes that they fantasize about, but are far-fetched and hardly achievable. This phrase was first coined by the Swedish-American activist, Joe Hill, in 1911. He was using it as a way of criticizing the Salvation Army's philosophy, especially when it came to saving the souls of the hungry rather than providing them food. Rather than actually helping them, they were providing them with an illusion of happiness or a "pie in the sky."

84. Bob's your uncle

The term "Bob's your uncle" is another way of saying "it's as simple as that!" We use this phrase to conclude an explanation of a set of simple instructions or when a result is reached. By using this idiom, we convey that we consider the instructions straightforward and understandable. The origin of the phrase was connected to the events involving the British Prime Minister Robert Gascoyne-Cecil in 1887. That year, Prime Minister Robert, whose nickname was Bob, appointed his nephew, Arthur James Balfour, as the Minister of Ireland. For Arthur, it was simple to advance in position and status because "Bob was his uncle!" However, there is a big time lapse between these events and the popularization of this phrase, so the theory is far from confirmed.

85. All ears

The expression "I'm all ears!" means that someone is listening intently to what is being said and is dedicating their full attention to it. We use this phrase when we want to state that our attention is focused on what the person is saying. Sometimes, saying "we're all ears" is a way of putting the person who's about to speak in the spotlight and letting them know that everyone in the room is going to be quiet and listen to what they have to say. This phrase originated in the 18th century.

86. Night owl

A person who stays up very late at night or who does their best work at night is called a "night owl." We use this expression to describe a person whose active period happens during the night, who likes staying awake when it's dark outside. This phrase comes from the patterns and habits of actual owls as they sleep during the day and hunt for food at night.

87. Jack of all trades

A "jack of all trades" is a person who is skilled in many different areas and can do various types of work. We use this idiom as a compliment for a versatile person who can always contribute, no matter what the task is. However, there is a longer version of this idiom - "Jack of all trades, master of none." In this form, the expression is less of a compliment, because it conveys that the person is interested in many different areas of expertise, but because they are so diverse in their interests, they never committed themselves enough to master one of those skills. The phrase stems from the 14th century and is found in John Gower's poem *Confessio Amantis*.

88. CHEW THE FAT

To "chew the fat" means to converse in a prolonged way and to take pleasure in it. It's usually a pleasant conversation between friends and acquaintances. For example, it's used when friends are gossiping together or telling stories from their pasts, and so on. There are multiple connections between this phrase and its origins. Chewing actual animal fat was done leisurely by the Northern American Native Americans. Farmers in Britain would also chew on pork fat when they were sitting and talking to others. It is even said that sailors did the same thing as a means of passing the time.

89. On the Mend

To mend something is to fix it, so if something is "on the mend," it means that it is either getting repaired or getting better. It usually refers to someone's health improving, but it can also be applied to other concepts, like when something that had deteriorated is in the process of getting back to its usual state, usually relationships between people. The idiom is based on the word "mend" which means "to repair" or "remove defects" and originates from the 13th century. This idiom has been applied with its meaning of improving health since the 1600s. It started to be used to describe an improvement in people's relationships in the 19th century.

90. Jump the Gun

To "jump the gun" means to act before one is supposed to or to do something too early without thinking it through first. We use this idiom to describe a person's hasty or reckless action or behavior. It is believed that this phrase is related to a gun being fired as a signal for the start of foot races or horse races. Competitors who started the race before the gun was fired were disqualified because they "jumped the gun" and went too early.

Did you know?

Even though we associate Cleopatra with ancient Egypt, she actually lived during times that were closer to the invention of smartphones than the construction of the pyramids. Wooly mammoths were still walking around at the time when the Great Pyramid of Giza was finished.

The first ever decree about human rights was issued by Persian King Cyrus the Great in 539 B.C. The decree established the freeing of slaves, declared that all people had the right to choose their own religion, and established racial equality.

Cats walk like camels and giraffes: they move both of their right feet first, then move both of their left feet. No other animals walk this way.

Our brains have a primal gaze detection system that determines whether someone is staring directly at us or not. So next time you feel that someone is watching you, they probably are.

91. Halfway house

A "halfway house" is a term used to describe the midway point in a process. However, there is a second, more literal meaning of the phrase. Namely, "halfway house" is a center for the rehabilitation of people who lived in various institutions - former convicts, psychiatric patients, and other members of the society who are unaccustomed to life outside an institution. This phrase was first recorded in the 17th century. There is a story related to the phrase of a British public house that existed in the 1600s. This house was known as the *Old Red Lion Inn* and it was used by the young Princess Victoria as a halfway point between her voyages.

92. Bull's eye

When someone hits a "bull's eye," they hit the very center of a target. This phrase can be used as a literal term in target practice, or it can be used to describe a situation when a person answers a question or handles a situation perfectly. The term originated from 19th-century English shooting contests, probably because the black spot in the center of the target resembled the eye of a bull. The circles around the center represented how far the contestants were from the intended target or the center of the board. The shooter who hit the center was considered to have hit the "bull's eye."

93. On a Tear

The expression "on a tear" has multiple applications. Americans consider being "on a tear" as achieving great success continually, in which case they say that the person has been "on a tear" lately. The British meaning of doing something "on a tear" translates to doing something very quickly or having a sudden burst of energy. Its third, rarest use, is related to describing someone who is drinking heavily. The phrase stems from the 19th century and was used to refer to someone who was on a "drunken tear," meaning they drink a lot and "tear up the town." However, the phrase diverged from the drinking context into its present interpretation.

94. Read between the lines

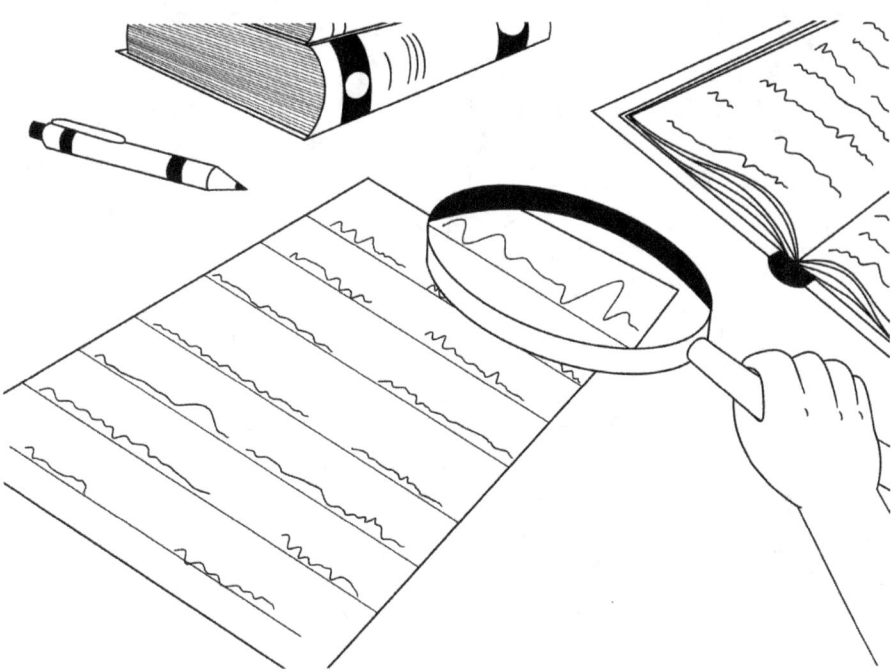

To "read between the lines" means to search for or find an implicit meaning of something written or said. We use this idiom to describe a situation when a message has more to tell us than the words on the surface. The implicit meaning that we are trying to point to is usually connected to people's real feelings or intentions that hide behind what they are saying. This expression derives from a simple form of cryptography in which a hidden meaning was conveyed by concealing it between lines of text.

95. Leg it

To "leg it" means to run very quickly, usually because the person running is being chased by someone else. We use this idiom to describe the action of running or fleeing, but also to invite someone to hurry up and start moving faster. The expression "use your legs" has been related to moving or speeding up one's movement since the 1500s. Over time, the phrase was shortened to just "leg it" as a quick way to tell someone to "move it."

96. Mum's the Word

The expression "mum's the word" can be translated as "be quiet" or "say nothing." Even though the term "mum" is most commonly used as a shortened version of the word "mother," in this context it is referring to humming, or the noise one makes with their mouth closed. The sound of humming indicates an unwillingness or inability to speak. Therefore, when someone says "mum's the word," its meaning is "shut your mouth" as you would when you are "humming."

97. Means to an End

A "means to an end" is something done as a step towards achieving an ultimate goal. Often, the phrase is used to convey an action that is done with only the end goal in mind and doesn't consider the potential harm that might be caused along the way. In many cases, using this phrase implies dishonesty and having secret agendas, because the person is behaving in a certain way or using someone else for their personal goals. This phrase is drawn back to the field of Economics. In early Economics, the resources of the Earth were called "means" while human needs were called "ends."

98. Devil's Advocate

When someone is playing "devil's advocate," they are acting as if they are on the opposite side of the discussion or the debate to promote thought or create an argument. It can also refer to being mischievous, confusing, and introducing opposing thoughts just for the sake of it. This phrase was first brought into English in the 18th century as it was derived from the Latin phrase "advocatus diaboli." The first time it was used in its modern form was in a humorous text titled *Impostors Detected* in 1760.

99. Once bitten twice shy

This proverb indicates that a negative experience causes people to be more cautious in the future. We use this proverbial saying in situations when people are being careful and guarded, so we assume that their past hurts or failures are the reason for it. A similar version of this proverb can be found in Eliza Fowler Haywood's novel *The History of Miss Betsy Thoughtless*, 1751, which quotes: "I have been bit once, and have made a vow never to settle upon any woman while I live, again."

100. TO THE NINES

"To the nines" can be translated as "to perfection" or "to the highest degree." We use this idiom to pay a compliment to how someone has completed something that they were aiming for and when we want to say "good job." In modern English, this compliment is most commonly paid regarding how the person is dressed; in such cases, we say that someone is "dressed to the nines" or "dressed up to the nines." The phrase is of Scottish origin. The earliest recorded sample of the expression is found in the 1719 *Epistle to Ramsay* by the Scottish poet William Hamilton.

101. WHEN IN ROME

The expression "when in Rome," which is followed by "do as Romans do," conveys that when a person is visiting a new place, they should follow the traditions of the culture that exists there. We often use this idiom in situations when a person is a tourist at a new and exotic destination with different customs, to encourage trying out new things. Furthermore, we can use it to state that a context or situation involves certain behavior and that it's for the best that we aspire to adapt to the context. The first printed use of this idiom can be traced back to 1777, in *Interesting Letters of Pope Clement XIV*.

Did you know?

In Greenland, the sun does not set from May 25th to July 25th. In the Arctic Circle, the midnight sun only lasts for about half an hour, but the further north you get, the longer it lasts. June 21, the longest day of the year, is a national holiday. July is the only month when Greenland's temperature reaches above freezing.

Chinese checkers wasn't actually invented in China, nor has a connection to any Asian country. The star-shaped marble game originated in Germany in 1892. When the game reached the United States, it started to be known as Chinese checkers, as American companies wanted to take advantage of the popularity of oriental imports.

The origin of the word "sinister" reflects a historical bias against left-handed people. It comes from the Latin word for "left," which was also seen to be unlucky or evil.

In the 1700s, coins were actually made of real gold and silver. Often criminals would shave down the sides of the coins and sell the shavings. Consequently, the US Mint began adding ridges to the coins, a process called reeding, to make it impossible to shave down without being detected, while also making counterfeiting more difficult. Today, no coins are made from precious metals, but the tradition has continued on coins of higher value. The reeding also helps the visually impaired to tell the difference between coins.

Bonus

Thanks for supporting me and purchasing this book! I'd like to send you some freebies. They include:

- The digital version of *500 World War I & II Facts*
- The digital version of *101 Idioms and Phrases*
- The audiobook for my best seller *1144 Random Facts*

Scan the QR code below, enter your email and I'll send you all the files. Happy reading!

Check out my other books!

www.ingramcontent.com/pod-product-compliance
Lightning Source LLC
Chambersburg PA
CBHW070046230426
43661CB00005B/777